T0268154

IMAGES
of America

GREAT
SALT LAKE

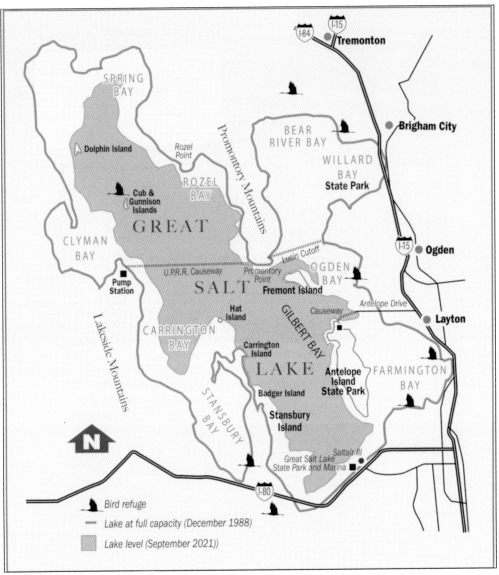

A modern map of the Great Salt Lake. (Courtesy of Robert Noyce.)

IMAGES
of America

GREAT
SALT LAKE

Lynn Arave and Ray Boren

ARCADIA
PUBLISHING

Published by Arcadia Publishing
Charleston, South Carolina

Printed in the United States of America

Library of Congress Control Number: 2022942326

For all general information, please contact Arcadia Publishing:
Telephone 843-853-2070
Fax 843-853-0044
E-mail sales@arcadiapublishing.com
For customer service and orders:
Toll-Free 1-888-313-2665

Visit us on the Internet at www.arcadiapublishing.com

We dedicate this book to Great Salt Lake's explorers, researchers, chroniclers, photographers, and advocates of the past, present, and future.

CONTENTS

ACKNOWLEDGMENTS

As a history- and photograph-oriented book, Images of America: *Great Salt Lake* would not have been possible without such resources as the Utah State Historical Society and its publications such as *Utah Historical Quarterly* and *History to Go* (a blog); the Utah Geological Survey; the Library of Congress; the archives of the Church of Jesus Christ of Latter-day Saints; and others across the United States. For their skills and help, special thanks go to Twila Van Leer, for reading and editing of the text; Robert Noyce, for his helpful maps; pilot Jerry Barfuss of Bountiful, Utah, whose generosity made many modern aerial photographs possible; Antelope Island State Park historian Carl Aldrich; and Adelaide H. Ryder and the Utah Museum of Fine Arts.

INTRODUCTION

On a map, and as seen from space, Utah's Great Salt Lake looks like a vast splotch, similar to a Rorschach inkblot test. That seems appropriate for the ancient but shrinking lake—a remnant of the Ice Age's much greater Lake Bonneville. It has meant many things to different people, from Native Americans and pioneer settlers to tourists, industrialists, and conservationists. It is certainly one of Utah's most distinctive landscapes, rivaled only by the state's red rock national parks and mountains with "the greatest snow on Earth."

But Great Salt Lake is in trouble. After hitting a record-high water level in the 1980s, it has been depleted by a decades-long drought, as well as ongoing diversion of tributary waters for human use. The lake's always-fluctuating shores have receded; its surface level is at historic lows. Scientists and lake advocates warn of catastrophes to come—from endangered creatures all along the food chain to toxic dust storms affecting nearby communities—if action is not taken.

Like its famed counterpart in the Middle East, Great Salt Lake is often called a "dead sea." As a terminal lake, with no outlet connecting it to Earth's oceans, its environs can be more desolate than the Great Basin deserts that bound much of it. Yet, it is not truly dead. Few species thrive in the saline lake itself; though, tiny brine shrimp, brine flies, and salt-adapted algae and bacteria are abundant. The lake's fresher margins and rivers, however, are havens to millions of migrating birds, native fish, and other life—including humans, whose communities approach its shores.

Eagles and other raptors patrol its fringes, which are shared with a bird-watcher's dream of bird life, from avocets and meadowlarks to red-winged blackbirds. Hunters tracking ducks and other waterfowl probe the marshes. Photographers anticipate vibrant sunsets and sunrises. Sailboats and kayaks offer adventure and solitude. Islands and promontories promise a rustic experience.

And—as declared on many an old postcard—swimmers and bathers testing Great Salt Lake's dense waters can still "float like a cork!"

Nevertheless, for much of the past century, Utahns and visitors alike have not seemed excited about bobbing in Great Salt Lake. Even though it is a starkly beautiful "great lake," the inconsistent coastlines, "lake stink" (usually a result of organic matter mixing with its briny edges), and lack of idyllic beaches and forested shores have made this inland sea sparingly visited and often ignored.

That was not the case in the 19th century and early decades of the 20th, when beaches and resorts thrived, drawing travelers from around the world. Among them was naturalist John Muir, who visited the south shore's Lake Point in 1877, and took a dip there, as reported in the *Salt Lake Herald*.

"When the north wind blows," Muir wrote for the newspaper, "bathing in (Great) Salt Lake is a glorious baptism, for then it is all wildly awake with waves, blooming like a prairie in snowy crystal foam. Plunging confidently into the midst of the grand uproar you are hugged and welcomed and swim without effort, rocking and whirling up and down and round in delightful rhythm while the wind sings in chorus and the cool, fragrant brine searches every fibre of your body, and at the end of your excursion you are tossed ashore with a glad God-speed, braced and salted and clean as a saint."

Muir was not the first nor the last to come away refreshed, if a bit salty; for despite Great Salt Lake's desiccated setting, to Native Americans and mountain men alike, as well as to immigrants, it was, and is, an oasis.

Indeed, well before Utah was "Utah," to mountaineer Jedediah Smith, Great Salt Lake meant "home." After traversing much of the West and blazing a path to Mexican California in 1826, Smith and two companions crossed the Sierra Nevada in 1827. They passed through the sage and alkaline valleys of what are today's Nevada and western Utah in a near-fatal eastward trek toward a rendezvous at Bear Lake. Upon glimpsing what trappers sometimes called the "big salt lake," a thirsty, exhausted Smith felt he had reached a sanctuary.

"Those who may chance to read this at a distance from the scene," he wrote in his journal, "may perhaps be surprised that the sight of this lake surrounded by a wilderness more than 2,000 miles in diameter excited in me those feelings known to the traveler, who, after long and perilous journeying, comes again in view of his home. But so it was with me for I had traveled so much in the vicinity of the Salt Lake that it had become my home of the wilderness."

To later topographers and scientists such as US Army surveyor captain Howard Stansbury, Great Salt Lake also proved a contradiction. Stansbury discovered, during an expedition in 1849 and 1850, not only desolation around the inland sea, with its "bleak and naked shores," but also "a great and peculiar beauty."

Stansbury added greatly to knowledge about the lake, for which the modern basics go something like this: Great Salt Lake is what hydrologists and geologists call an endorheic or terminal lake—the in-flowing waters stop here, on the eastern frontier of North America's Great Basin at the base of the Wasatch Mountains, an outlying range of the Rocky Mountains. Despite myths and early map-makers' expectations of a river to the Pacific Ocean—the legendary (and nonexistent) Rio Buenaventura, or perhaps a whirlpool—it has no outlet. Great Salt Lake is, the Utah Geological Survey reports, about 35 miles wide and 75 miles long, at an average elevation of 4,200 feet above sea level. However, due to fluctuations caused by wet years and dry ones, the lake's size varies significantly—20 feet or more between highs and lows. In peak years, as in the 1980s, Great Salt Lake covered 1,472,000 acres. At its lowest, as in recent years, the lake spans only half that, as the West experiences the most severe drought in hundreds of years.

Great Salt Lake is the biggest, fresh or saline, in the United States, after the Great Lakes. It contains about 4.5 to 4.9 billion tons of dissolved salt. Historically, its salinity has ranged from 5 percent—slightly higher than sea water—to 27 percent, a point beyond which water cannot hold more salt. That saltiness is what makes swimmers so buoyant.

With its impressive vistas and factoids, and considering Utah's bounty of national parks (Arches, Bryce Canyon, Canyonlands, Capitol Reef, and Zion), national monuments, and other spotlighted landscapes, it seems surprising that Great Salt Lake is not among their number. Bird and wildlife refuges do skirt its edges, and Utah has established Great Salt Lake State Park and Antelope Island State Park.

Yet, there is no "Great Salt Lake National Park."

Not that the idea has not come up. In the 1960s, Utah's then US senator Frank Moss proposed such a park. He did not envision the entire lake being set aside, but Moss told the *Weekly Reflex*, a newspaper, that he liked the idea of portions being set aside. He was open to ideas about impounding freshwater bays and considering other recreational concepts. But the senator's proposal, and others, never gained traction.

Even so, Great Salt Lake remains one of the wonders of Utah, the United States, and the world.

One

EARLY HISTORY
AND EXPLORATION

Great Salt Lake is a remnant of an even greater inland sea, now called Lake Bonneville. During the Ice Age, Lake Bonneville filled a basin that stretched from today's Utah-Idaho border to southwestern Utah. At its greatest extent, it was 346 miles long and 145 miles wide. Imagine superimposing such a lake upon Utah's modern landscape. At its highest level, Lake Bonneville would have drowned Salt Lake City under a thousand feet of fresh water.

Geologist Grove Karl Gilbert recognized that a prehistoric lake had filled Utah's valleys and gave its terraces names, including Bonneville, Provo, and Stansbury. Rising Lake Bonneville reached its maximum depth about 14,500 years ago. It breached an unstable barrier at Idaho's Red Rock Pass, initiating a torrent—the Bonneville Flood—that rushed into the Snake River watershed to the northwest, then the Columbia River, and finally the Pacific Ocean. That release, and a warming climate, initiated Lake Bonneville's decline. The water, in a smaller and smaller pool, became saltier and mineral laden, and Great Salt Lake was born.

Ancient Native Americans lived along Great Salt Lake's shores. Their presence, even 11,000 years ago, has been confirmed at archaeological sites such as Danger Cave and the Promontory Caves. Spanish missionary-explorers Atanasio Dominguez and Silvestre Velez de Escalante encountered tribes in 1776 during an expedition out of Santa Fe, seeking a route to California. The friars made it to Utah Lake but did not see the bigger lake.

The first European American to visit Great Salt Lake may have been frontiersman Jim Bridger in 1825. Bridger thought the salty waters to be the edge of the Pacific Ocean. The first US government expedition to the lake was led by John C. Fremont in 1843, with a company that included guide Kit Carson. Pioneer wagons reconnoitered the lake's edges in the early 1840s, and the ill-fated Donner Party, headed to California, passed the south shore in 1846. One year later, Mormon pioneers entered the Salt Lake Valley and founded Utah's first major modern settlement—Great Salt Lake City.

In the early 1930s, University of Utah anthropologist Julian H. Steward and crews explored the Promontory Caves on Great Salt Lake's north shore. They discovered about 250 moccasins and leather pieces, as well as pottery, arrow shafts and points, and stone tools. Carbon-dated from 1150 AD to the late 1200s, the items are attributed to Athabaskan or Dene/Navajo people migrating from Canada. (Courtesy of J. Willard Marriott Library, University of Utah.)

A photograph from student Omer C. Stewart's collection shows archaeological work in 1931 at a cave, likely on Utah's Promontory Peninsula, under the direction Julian H. Steward, a University of Utah anthropology professor, cosponsored by the Smithsonian Institute's Bureau of American Ethnology. Steward's explorations there, and at other sites, preceded his 1937 report "Ancient Caves of the Great Salt Lake Region." (Courtesy of J. Willard Marriott Library, University of Utah.)

A map created in the 1960s by historian David E. Miller illustrates how large Great Salt Lake's precursor Lake Bonneville was. Its vanished stems and bays overlay the modern state of Utah. Lake Bonneville was in places 1,000 feet deep and stretched into today's southern Idaho and eastern Nevada. (Courtesy of Utah State Historical Society.)

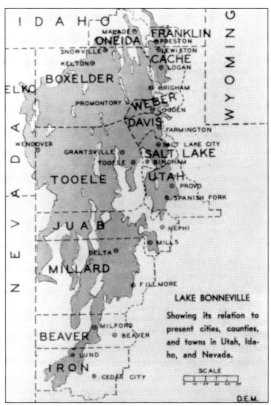

Red Rock Pass in southern Idaho is where Lake Bonneville spilled over and began to drain into the Snake River watershed, some 14,500 years ago. This 2014 photograph shows where the Cache Valley meets Marsh Valley. Farming is a dominant feature here now, and the pass hosts a railroad line and the highway US 91. The pass is named for red limestone cliffs in the area. (Ray Boren photograph.)

Ancient Lake Bonneville began its long decline when water breached a natural but unstable barrier at Red Rock Pass and Marsh Valley, pictured here in a 2014 photograph. The resulting Bonneville Flood rushed into the Portneuf and Snake River corridors to the Columbia River and thence to the Pacific Ocean. Before the catastrophic Bonneville Flood, the pass was about 300 feet higher than it is now. (Ray Boren photograph.)

The shoreline of ancient Lake Bonneville is visible on the lower slopes of the Wasatch Mountains of Cache Valley in this 1940 photograph. Like bathtub rings, the highest level of the 1,000-foot-deep lake is indelibly marked above this rural setting. (Courtesy of Utah State Historical Society.)

A statue of Capt. Benjamin L.E. Bonneville, for whom Lake Bonneville is named, is part of a monument at Salt Lake City's This Is the Place Heritage Park, which honors native peoples, explorers, and settlers. Geologist G.K. Gilbert named the prehistoric lake in Bonneville's honor, even though Bonneville probably never saw Great Salt Lake. A US Army officer on leave, Bonneville explored the West in the early 1830s. (Ray Boren photograph.)

A portrait of legendary mountain men and traders Jim Bridger and Louis Vasquez welcomes visitors as part of a display in the museum at Fort Bridger State Historic Site in southwestern Wyoming. The two men founded the fort in 1843 as a supply stop along the Oregon Trail. The far-ranging Bridger, known as "Old Gabe," may have been the first European American to see Great Salt Lake in 1824. (Ray Boren photograph.)

A photograph taken for the Clarence King–led US Geological Survey of the Fortieth Parallel, also known as the King Survey, shows the upper Bear River in Utah's Uinta Mountains. The image, by Timothy H. O'Sullivan, an important chronicler of the Civil War, is from between 1867 and 1872. The Bear River is the principal tributary flowing into Great Salt Lake. (Courtesy of National Archives.)

For many in the 19th century, the first depictions the general public saw of Great Salt Lake were images such as this lithograph, created by the printmaking firm Currier & Ives. The fanciful original presents a large mountain-bordered lake, with Salt Lake City right on its shores. (Currier and Ives, American, *Great Salt Lake, Utah*, before 1872, hand-colored lithograph. From the Permanent Collection of the Utah Museum of Fine Arts.)

Brigham Young, president of the Church of Jesus Christ of Latter-day Saints, poses for an 1865 photograph by Charles William Carter. Young led colonization of Great Salt Lake Valley, as well as the wider Great Basin. He was well aware of Great Salt Lake's potential before he led the Mormon pioneers westward, having studied the journals of earlier explorers, notably John C. Fremont's government reports. (Courtesy of National Portrait Archives.)

Brigham Young and Pioneers Entering the Valley is among the historic murals encircling the rotunda inside Utah State Capitol. Featuring the pioneer Mormon leader, it represents the 1847 arrival of settlers in Salt Lake Valley. The colorful mural was created by Lee Greene Richards, with assistance from Gordon H. Cope, Waldo P. Midgley, and Harry Rasmussen, in 1933–1934. (Ray Boren photograph.)

A lithograph from the 1850s presents a view west of Promontory Point over Great Salt Lake. The illustration was created for topographical engineer captain Howard Stansbury's US Army report detailing his exploration and survey of the valley of the Great Salt Lake of Utah. (Courtesy of Library of Congress.)

Thomas Moran painted this high view of horsemen cresting a pass above Great Salt Lake in the 1870s. Famous for his epic paintings of Yellowstone and the Grand Canyon, Moran visited Utah to join a party led by explorer John Wesley Powell. (Courtesy of the Library of Congress.)

Great Salt Lake's Black Rock and nearby slopes take on a rugged yet romantic aspect in Alfred Lambourne's 19th-century landscape painting. The artist also rendered scenes in Yellowstone, the Grand Canyon, and Yosemite, as well as Utah mountains and canyons. (Alfred Lambourne, American, *Black Rock, Great Salt Lake*, 1887, oil on canvas. From the Permanent Collection of the Utah Museum of Fine Arts.)

The bones of a large animal, possibly a horse, are recorded in this early-20th-century photograph in the Great Salt Lake Desert. Though crossed by wagon trains and immigrants headed to California, the area is dry and inhospitable. Water sources are scarce, and summer temperatures are scorching. (Courtesy of Utah State Historical Society.)

A US Army truck is mired in salt flats in a 1919 photograph by Sgt. S.C. Lacy. Testing men and vehicles, including trucks, motorcycles, and ambulances, the Army's Motor Transport Corps crossed the nation from Washington, DC, to San Francisco, often along the early Lincoln Highway. The route, which traversed 3,251 rough miles in 62 days, included a passage south and west of Great Salt Lake. (Courtesy of Library of Congress.)

Among the 282 officers and enlisted men participating in the 1919 Motor Transport Corps convoy was Lt. Col. Dwight D. Eisenhower, who observed the often impassable roads and transport breakdowns. Decades later, the convoy's struggles, and his experiences commanding Allied forces in Europe during World War II, prompted Eisenhower—elected president of the United States in 1953—to authorize the Interstate Highway System. (Courtesy of the Library of Congress.)

Two

ANTELOPE ISLAND

At 28,000 acres, Antelope Island is the largest isle in Great Salt Lake. A state park, it is prized for its accessible, yet "outback" atmosphere; for outstanding vistas; and for the driving, hiking, running, biking, and horseback-riding recreation it affords.

Before pioneer settlers arrived, John C. Fremont again visited the region in 1845. Native Americans told him about the big island, so Fremont's party splashed their way to it across a sandbar. They found grass, fresh water, and pronghorn antelope. A few animals were hunted, so Fremont named the island for them, "in memory of the grateful supply of food they furnished." According to historian Dale L. Morgan, one indigenous man claimed ownership of the island and challenged Fremont's hunting there.

After 1847, it was generally called "Church Island" because the Church of Jesus Christ of Latter-day Saints was granted ownership on behalf of an emigration fund. The church grazed herds of horses, as well as cattle and sheep, there. A dozen American bison—buffalo—were transported to the island in 1893 and flourished. Today's herd ranges from 550 to 700 animals. Each autumn, a round-up is staged to gather the bison, check their health, and sell extra animals to control the herd's size.

The island had at least one resident before Mormon settlers arrived: Daddy Stump, a mountain man, who subsequently moved on. Virginia native Fielding Garr was the first permanent Mormon settler, arriving in 1848 as church ranch foreman. A widower, his children joined him in 1849. Garr's adobe-brick house remains today, serving as a museum. Others also homesteaded on the island, including the family of George and Alice Frary. In 1870, the isle was purchased by John Dooly Sr., who operated the Island Improvement Company.

In 1969, after the seven-mile Davis County Causeway was constructed, the state opened a northern portion of Antelope Island as a district of Great Salt Lake State Park. In 1981, the state purchased the entire island for what then became Antelope Island State Park. The park features a visitor center, the historic Garr Ranch, a marina, a seasonal grill, multiple campgrounds, sandy beaches, and many trails.

This entrance sign welcomed visitors at the start of the causeway to Antelope Island in the mid-1970s. The Davis County Causeway washed out in the 1980s. Antelope Island opened to the driving public in 1969 as a unit of Great Salt Lake State Park. Only the north tip could be visited, as the rest was in private ownership. In 1981, the full island was purchased by the state. (Lynn Arave photograph.)

Explorer John C. Fremont named Antelope Island for the pronghorn, a small, horned, deer-sized ungulate that is not actually an antelope, which are Old World species. Fremont and his party splashed their way to the island in 1845 on horseback along a sandbar, looked around, and killed some pronghorn antelope for food. (Ray Boren photograph.)

A battered, bullet-peppered sign warns trespassers to keep off private property on Antelope Island. The Island Improvement Company, later the Island Ranching Company, owned almost all of the island, and ran sheep and cattle from 1884 to 1972. The sign is displayed today at the state park's historic Fielding Garr Ranch. (Ray Boren photograph.)

In a mid-20th-century aerial photograph taken before the isle became a state park, Fielding Garr Ranch spreads across a sloping plain on Antelope Island's southeastern shore. Corrals and a long shed are to the north. The largest building is a sheep-shearing shed. The ranch house is visible to the left of a grove of tall trees, which engulf a natural spring. (Courtesy of the Max Harward Collection, Antelope Island State Park.)

Sheep became the primary inhabitants of Antelope Island around the turn of the 20th century. By then, the entire island was owned by businessman John Dooly Sr. and his Island Improvement Company. The herder in this undated photograph has wrapped a bandanna around his head, perhaps to ward off gnats and biting flies, often dubbed "no-see-ums," which cause misery in springtime. (Courtesy of the Max Harward Collection, Antelope Island State Park.)

Under John Dooly Jr., the sheep herd expanded to 10,000 animals, making Antelope Island one of the major ranching enterprises in the United States. Several springs provide water on the island, but getting it to the thirsty and far-ranging sheep proved a challenge, as is evident in this undated photograph. (Courtesy of the Max Harward Collection, Antelope Island State Park.)

Although horses, hogs, cattle, and chickens were also raised on Antelope Island, sheep dominated for decades. Part of the ranch routine was shearing them, as in this mid-20th-century photograph. The wool market declined in the 1950s, so the operation turned to cattle. In 1981, the state, which had owned the northern 2,000 acres since 1969, bought the rest of Antelope Island. (Courtesy of the Max Harward Collection, Antelope Island State Park.)

Almost from the beginning of settlement, the Church of Jesus Christ of Latter-day Saints kept horses and cattle on isolated Antelope Island—then often called "Church Island." A log cabin was built in 1848. Fielding Garr, who managed the early herds, soon after built an adobe-brick house, which is to the left in this photograph from the early 1920s. (Courtesy of the Max Harward Collection, Antelope Island State Park.)

Black Rock is a landmark on Great Salt Lake, south of Antelope Island, visible here in the background. The image, created by photographer C.R. Savage (1832–1909), is likely from the 1880s, before the lake level dropped for several years. Familiar to early wagon trains and settlers, Black Rock can be seen and visited today, though it is no longer an islet. (Courtesy of the Church of Jesus Christ of Latter-day Saints.)

Three wooden boats float beside Elephant Head, a formation on Antelope Island's northwest side, in 1916. The landform looks much like an elephant, including its trunk, from certain perspectives, as from Buffalo Point above White Rock Bay. The names Buffalo Island and Antelope Island were used interchangeably for many years. Antelope prevailed, even though buffalo (bison) were introduced beginning in the 1890s. (Courtesy of Utah State Historical Society.)

An early aerial photograph of Great Salt Lake highlights the southern end of Antelope Island. The picture was taken by Capt. A.W. Stevens in 1925. Antelope is the lake's largest island, encompassing 42 square miles. It is often connected to the mainland when the lake's level is low, as has been the case in recent years. (Courtesy of Library of Congress.)

Antelope Island and Great Salt Lake sprawl in the distance, beyond bustling Salt Lake City and its western neighborhoods, in a 1930s image captured from an airplane. Except for scattered resorts and grazing lands, the lake's fluctuating levels and muddy wetlands generally kept settlers and urban development from encroaching upon the uncertain shorelines. (Courtesy of Utah Historical Society.)

A pastoral 1938 photograph from the Bountiful foothills highlights Antelope Island to the west. Although it is essentially a desert island, there are springs. Fielding Garr Ranch, not distinctly visible across the water to the left, had the most reliable source, and thus, it became the focus of sheep and cattle operations that flourished for more than a century. (Courtesy of Utah State Historical Society.)

The *Covered Wagon*, a 1923 silent film considered to be the first epic Western movie, was filmed in part on Antelope Island. The director was James Cruze, a native of Ogden, Utah. A key scene, a buffalo hunt and stampede, was staged on an east-side slope, now known as Camera Flat, using the island's bison herd, which then had about 200 animals. (Paramount Pictures.)

Utah governor George Dern participated in a buffalo hunt on Antelope Island in 1926, and he was successful. However, many Utahns and out-of-staters protested that hunt. Dern maintained that both the island and the herd were privately owned and that the state of Utah had no control over such a private hunt. (Courtesy of Utah State Historical Society.)

Horses were occasionally used to cross Great Salt Lake to Fremont and Antelope Islands when water levels were low, mostly to check on livestock. This 1943 photograph shows horses on the sandbar leading to Fremont Island. These horses were being used on the isle to track down a pesky coyote responsible for killing livestock there; unfortunately, he evaded hunters for weeks. (Courtesy of Utah State Historical Society.)

Charles Stoddard of West Point, Utah, stands on a rare "iceberg" in the Great Salt Lake. Stoddard reported that this stack, in 1942, was 30 feet high and 100 feet square. Ice can form in shallows along Great Salt Lake's shores, where incoming fresh water has not yet been diluted with salt. Vigorous winds can then shatter and drive the ice into tall piles. (Courtesy of Utah State Historical Society.)

John C. Fremont visited the island in 1843 with Kit Carson, becoming the first known European Americans to do so. Fremont's career proved mercurial. Claiming control of California while a US Army major during the Mexican-American War, he endured a court martial. He became rich during the Gold Rush. He was military governor of California, Arizona's territorial governor, and served in the Civil War. (Courtesy of the Library of Congress.)

Three

FREMONT AND
OTHER ISLES

Around a campfire in 1843, after their first good look at Great Salt Lake, explorer John C. Fremont and his men speculated about the trees and game they hoped to find when they ventured in a frail cloth boat to an island close by.

Fremont came away calling it "Disappointment Island." While boating in 1848, pioneer Albert Carrington and friends named it "Castle Island." Later, Capt. Howard Stansbury, a topographer, bestowed its enduring name, Fremont Island, honoring his predecessor.

Fremont was not entirely crestfallen by what he found. When he and his crew arrived, they climbed a rocky point. "Standing on the summit, we enjoyed an extended view of the lake, enclosed in a basin of rugged mountains," he wrote. His companion, guide Kit Carson, apparently bored, chiseled a crude cross on a rock.

During the spring of 1859, Henry W. Jacob and Dan Miller put 153 head of sheep on the isle. They called it "Miller's Island." That one did not stick either.

Over the years, Fremont Island continued to generate tales. Jean Baptiste, a Salt Lake City Cemetery worker, was arrested for robbing graves, taking clothes, and jewelry. He was exiled to Fremont Island in 1862. Baptiste escaped and was never heard from again. From 1886 to 1891, ailing judge Uriah J. Wenner lived on Fremont with his family. He is buried there. Peter G. Czerny, author of *The Great Great Salt Lake*, said of Fremont Island, "For even though the island is barren it has a magical quality, and those who have visited it have never lost the desire to return to it."

The Utah Geological Survey says the lake has 17 named islands and islets, notably Stansbury, usually a promontory, and Carrington, named for pioneer Albert Carrington, who assisted Stansbury. Some, like Badger Island, vanish when the lake rises, and Strong's Knob and Cub Island divide into islets. These and others, like Hat Island, sit on plains when water is low. A few of the smallest are among the best known, including Egg Island and White Rock, near Antelope Island, and Black Rock, off Great Salt Lake's south shore.

A 1962 photograph shows an old corral on Fremont Island's east side. Exotic sheep, cattle, horses—even a small herd of Shetland ponies—grazed on the island over the decades. In the distance is the isle's highest point, Castle Rock. (Courtesy of Utah State Historical Society.)

This portrait depicts John Charles Fremont, for whom Fremont Island is named. Employing a frail boat, on September 9, 1843, Fremont and members of his expedition landed on and explored the island. Fremont himself dubbed it "Disappointment Island" for its lack of game and foliage. In 1856, the year this lithograph was published, he was the first-ever Republican party nominee for president of the United States. (Courtesy of Library of Congress.)

Earl Stoddard points to a legendary cross that Kit Carson carved on a Fremont Island rock face in 1843. A cousin of sheep rancher Charles Stoddard, who leased the island, he was likely visiting in the 1930s. The cross was a mystery until 1926, when Carson's life story was published. Before that, no one knew how old the cross was or who carved it. (Courtesy of Utah State Historical Society.)

Pictured in 1868, Christopher "Kit" Carson was a member of John C. Fremont's 1843 expedition. Already famous at the time, Carson was one of the best-known trappers and explorers of the American West. He was a principal guide for three of Fremont's five exploratory treks through the American West. (Courtesy of Library of Congress.)

An undated photograph, probably from the 1940s, shows what was left of the Wenner family's house on Fremont Island. Uriah J. Wenner, an attorney and probate judge in Salt Lake City, was afflicted with tuberculosis. He, his wife, Kate, and their children moved to the island in 1886 to try to improve his health. He died there in 1891, and the family moved away. (Courtesy of Utah State Historical Society.)

Another photograph, also likely from the 1940s, captures the time-worn Wenner home on Fremont Island. By the 1980s, the structure had been leveled by storms and lack of maintenance, and all that remained was a foundation embedded in the ground. Wagon wheels, perhaps from the 19th century, and other remnants litter the foreground. (Courtesy of Utah State Historical Society.)

The gravesite of Uriah J. Wenner and his wife, Kate, on Fremont Island, was photographed in 1959. Uriah's widow, Kate Wenner Noble, remarried after his death, but when she died 51 years later, her ashes were buried here next to her first husband. (Courtesy of Utah State Historical Society.)

A metal grave marker remembering the Wenners is attached to a rock monument on the southwest side of Fremont Island. The house where the couple and their children lived during the 1880s and early 1890s is located a few hundred yards away, on Fremont's southeast side. (Lynn Arave photograph.)

New trees and a garden were planted on Fremont Island as part of a 1962 experiment. Water was diverted from a spring into a small canal. The fence was intended to keep livestock away. The experiment did not succeed, and today there are still only a few trees on the island. (Courtesy of Utah State Historical Society.)

A 1942 photograph shows Charles Stoddard's legendary "lakemobile" in Great Salt Lake. The truck, used on a sandbar route to Fremont Island where Stoddard kept livestock, had become trapped in mucky water the year prior. The rancher returned in the late spring to restart and move it. Although the vehicle was caked with salt, he did manage to start it. (Courtesy of Utah State Historical Society.)

A boat named *Hydrographer* sits off the northeast shore of Fremont Island on November 21, 1932. The motorboat was manned by four men—Jones, Freeman, Sims, and Adams (first names unknown). With more than 2,900 acres, Fremont is a larger island than it appears from the Wasatch Front. A large section not visible from the east juts westward. (Courtesy of Utah State Historical Society.)

Fremont Island, topped by Castle Rock, lies in silhouette off Promontory Point, the Promontory Peninsula's southernmost tip, as viewed in this 2009 photograph taken from Antelope Island. Long privately owned, Fremont Island was purchased in 2020 by the Nature Conservancy, which then handed it over to the State of Utah. A conservation easement allows public access, but only for such activities as hiking, biking, picnicking, and bird-watching. (Ray Boren photograph.)

The southwestern shores and terraced slopes of Great Salt Lake's Stansbury Island rise from a maze of evaporative ponds in this aerial photograph from 2009. An unpaved public road follows the shoreline to the northern tip, and trails offer hikers access to some benches and summits, but much of the island is in private ownership. The island is named for Capt. Howard Stansbury. (Ray Boren photograph.)

Apparently taken from a boat, this undated photograph highlights the choppy waters of Great Salt Lake, with rugged Stansbury Island in the background. Sudden squalls, especially in the 19th century, caused many shipwrecks, and prompted woeful tales of sea-sickness. Kate Wenner, for one, wrote that stormy weather made her family's first voyage to Fremont Island in 1886 a wet and exhausting three-day ordeal. (Courtesy of Utah State Historical Society.)

An aerial photograph, taken from a military aircraft in 1929, offers a vantage of the southwestern Great Salt Lake and Stansbury Island. The island—most often a mountainous peninsula—was named during his 1850 government survey. It was also briefly known as Kimball's Island, for Heber C. Kimball, a pioneer settler and leader, who had livestock there. (Courtesy of Library of Congress.)

A small boat approaches Cub Island in November 1934. Located off Gunnison Island's north tip, in Great Salt Lake's northwestern arm, Cub becomes a part of Gunnison during low water levels. As a result, it is perceived as the "offspring" of Gunnison. Many bird species nest on the islands, so access is restricted to protect rookeries, particularly for the American white pelican. (Courtesy of Utah State Historical Society.)

Charles Stoddard of West Point, Utah, pauses at the door of his small cabin on Carrington Island in 1936. Stoddard explored much of the Great Salt Lake and raised livestock in the region. Carrington Island, which lies north of Stansbury Island and west of Antelope Island, was named by Capt. Howard Stansbury for Albert Carrington, an assistant during Stansbury's 1849–1850 expedition. (Courtesy of Utah State Historical Society.)

Game hunters J.E. Jones and Stanley Evans pose beside a rock mound on Carrington Island, in October 1933. Howard Stansbury's men built the stack during a two-year topographical survey of Great Salt Lake, Utah Lake, and the Jordan River, which connects them. Stansbury's report, *Exploration and Survey of the Valley of the Great Salt Lake of Utah,* in short, was published in 1853. (Courtesy of Utah State Historical Society.)

Possibly in the 1920s, men pose on Bird Island, known today as Hat Island. The isle was at times named for birds that roost there. However, during low water it is linked to the mainland by dry lake bed, and predators such as coyotes drive birds away. It is now the state's Hat Island Wildlife Management Area, protecting pelicans, terns, great blue herons, and other species. (Courtesy of Utah State Historical Society.)

Disturbed gulls take flight as a man approaches nests on Egg Island in 1907. Howard Stansbury and his men named the island in 1850, when they harvested 76 heron eggs there. The small island is just west of Antelope Island's Ladyfinger Point. Because access is easy when the lake bed is dry, Antelope Island State Park asks today's visitors not to disturb nesting species. (Courtesy of Utah State Historical Society.)

Gunnison Island, shown in a photograph of uncertain date, is named for the Stansbury Expedition's second in command, Lt. John W. Gunnison. A topographical crew set up a triangulation station there in 1850 as part of their mapping effort. Artist Alfred Lambourne tried to homestead and establish a vineyard on the island in 1895–1896 and worked on a book, *Our Inland Sea*. (Courtesy of Antelope Island State Park.)

Birds are Gunnison Island's primary visitors and inhabitants. Today, the 155-acre island is off-limits, managed by the Utah Division of Wildlife Resources as a refuge and rookery for American white pelicans, where the birds nest and raise their young. Unfortunately, Great Salt Lake's low water levels and drying lake bed allow coyotes and other predators access, and the pelican population has dropped. (Courtesy of Antelope Island State Park.)

Four

PLEASURE AND THE BRINE

According to the 2020 US Census, more than 2.6 million people live along Utah's Wasatch Front near or beside Great Salt Lake. Most have never dipped a toe in it. That was not always the case. In days of yore, the lake was a source of fascination and pleasure. Only days after entering Salt Lake Valley, a few of the first Mormon pioneers wasted little time heading out to swim in the briny lake.

According to Milton R. Hunter, in his 1956 book, *Utah in Her Western Setting*, on July 27, 1847, a dozen settlers journeyed to the lake's south shore to check it out. They called the spot "Black Rock," after a landmark, ate lunch, and took a swim. Orson Pratt reported the following: "We cannot sink in this water. We roll and float on the surface like a dry log. I think the Salt Lake is one of the wonders of the world."

Beaches, bathhouses, and resorts developed in succeeding decades. But boating, canoeing, and kayaking are among the most delightful ways to experience Great Salt Lake.

Mountain men such as Jim Bridger and James Clyman are known to have used small craft during the 1820s, and John C. Fremont's party followed in 1843. Sailing craft made their debut in 1847 with the *Mud Hen*. Today, graceful sailboats catch the breezes and even race on the lake. Bases for such activities (water level permitting) include Great Salt Lake State Park and Marina, on the south shore, and Antelope Island State Park. Willard Bay Reservoir was created northeast of the lake to impound fresh water for irrigation and recreation. It, too, became a state park, a venue for boating, water skiing, and fishing.

Marathon swimming became a fad for a time at Great Salt Lake. "Annual marathon furnishes a thrill," read a 1920 newspaper headline. This, the "first annual" race, authorized by the US Amateur Athletic Union, started on Antelope Island and ended at Saltair.

Drier competition also took hold farther west. Utah's Salt Flats and the Bonneville Raceway, near Wendover, were to become the site of many world land speed records.

A pair of women enjoy the sand and sun, possibly after a swim, at Saltair's beach in an undated photograph. Early pioneer Orson Pratt said the following after a lake swim in 1847: "We cannot sink in this water. We roll and float on the surface like a dry log. I think the Salt Lake is one of the wonders of the world." (Courtesy of Library of Congress.)

Great Salt Lake was popular for more than swimming. Some resorts offered boat excursions and, eventually, other amenities. This craft, probably photographed in the 1890s, is beside a pier by Black Rock. The landmark was the first place where pioneer settlers swam and boated in the lake. However, when the new Saltair resort and pavilion opened nearby in the 1890s, interest in the location waned. (Courtesy of Utah State Historical Society.)

Heber C. Kimball, a Mormon pioneer and church leader, liked Great Salt Lake so much that he built this stone house on the south shore near Black Rock, visible in the background, by 1860. The building was later used by the Black Rock Resort. Another pioneer, Daniel H. Wells, also constructed a rock dwelling on the lake's shores in 1862. (Courtesy of the Church of Jesus Christ of Latter-day Saints.)

A small steamship is docked at a pier beside Black Rock in this 1885 drawing by Frenchman Albert Charles Tissandier. Bathing beaches and major resorts developed along Great Salt Lake's southern and eastern shores from the late 19th century through the first half of the 20th. (Albert Charles Tissandier, French, *Steamer at Bathing Pier*, 1885, pencil, ink, and paper. From the Permanent Collection of the Utah Museum of Fine Arts.)

This 1880s photograph shows the Garfield Resort on Great Salt Lake. Garfield Beach, also known as Garfield Landing, was the lake's premier resort from 1881 to 1893, until the even grander Saltair opened. Some 80,000 people visited Garfield in 1888. Its dance floor, 165 feet by 62 feet over the lake, was a principal attraction. Fire destroyed the resort in 1904. (Courtesy of the Church of Jesus Christ of Latter-day Saints.)

The steamboat *City of Corinne*, named for a railroad town north of Great Salt Lake, was one of the largest craft to ply the "inland sea." Launched in 1871 on the Bear River, it was 150 feet long, had three decks, and was built at a cost of $40,000. A 1904 fire burned the boat down to the water line. (Courtesy of the Church of Jesus Christ of Latter-day Saints.)

A group portrait shows boat passengers enjoying a day on Great Salt Lake. Even today, sailors rhapsodize about how pleasant an outing can be on the lake, with its reflective surface and sublime views. Yet, sudden storms can be a challenge on the shallow, saline waters. Dense, 10-foot waves can churn upward in minutes. (Courtesy of Utah State Historical Society.)

This undated photograph, perhaps from the early 1900s, shows people boarding an excursion boat on a rocky Great Salt Lake shore. Note the narrow planks being used to access the boat and women in full-length dresses who have obviously negotiated the passage, or are about to do so. (Courtesy of Utah State Historical Society.)

A crowded steamboat makes a landing, possibly at Antelope Island. This undated picture shows how well-dressed the passengers were in another time—the men are in suits and hats, and the women are in long dresses. Those on this pleasure cruise are believed to have traveled from Saltair to the island, perhaps in the 1920s. (Courtesy of Utah State Historical Society.)

In an undated antique photograph, a group of men is shown sailing on Great Salt Lake. All kinds of boats are permitted on the lake, but sailboats are common sights. Most watercraft past and present have sailed from the lake's accessible south shores. (Courtesy of Utah State Historical Society.)

Scottish American conservationist John Muir, famed for his advocacy of Yosemite Valley, California's Sierra Nevada range, and other wonders, visited Utah's Great Salt Lake on a cool, windy day in May 1877. The *Salt Lake Herald* headlined its newspaper report as follows: "Great Salt Lake. America's Dead Sea poetically pictured by a Naturalist. Prof. Muir's bath at Lake Point." (Courtesy of Library of Congress.)

Bobbing in salt-saturated Great Salt Lake was a popular pastime from pioneer days into the 20th century. In this stereoview from 1904, bathers stroll and float in shallows near Saltair's domed and turreted pavilion. Pioneer leaders and settlers first visited Great Salt Lake's southern beaches only days after they arrived in the Salt Lake Valley. (Courtesy of Library of Congress.)

A 1902 stereograph finds young people enjoying a pleasant day in and around a rowboat at Saltair. For those interested in more than simply bobbing and bathing, a boat would have been a good way to enjoy Great Salt Lake. Big-brimmed hats and long swimming attire were obviously the fashion at the time, for both modesty and protection from the sun and elements. (Courtesy of Library of Congress.)

Bathers enjoy a refreshing float in the Great Salt Lake in 1902, near Saltair. The *Deseret News* reported in 1907 that a man could sit in the lake's waters as a man sits in a rocking chair—suspended upward. The lake's early tourists noted that the water was so comfortably warm that they did not want to leave it. (Courtesy of Library of Congress.)

→ 30   → 30 A   → 31   → 31A   → 32   → 32 A

Sailboats dot Great Salt Lake in this sequence of contact prints, from negative film taken by a *Salt Lake Tribune* photographer in 1967. Although stymied in recent years by low water levels, sailing has been popular on the lake since the mid-19th century. Members of the Great Salt Lake Yacht Club, founded in 1877, proclaimed themselves to be "the world's saltiest sailors." (Courtesy of Utah State Historical Society.)

A photograph from the 1940s shows construction work on the Great Salt Lake Yacht Club marina, now part of the south shore's Great Salt Lake State Park. The first sailing boat on the lake, launched soon after pioneers arrived, was called the *Mud Hen*. It was 15 feet long and floated the lake beginning in 1847 or 1848. (Courtesy of Utah State Historical Society.)

A lone marathon swimmer, possibly E.C. Watson, races from Antelope Island to Black Rock in an 8.16-mile contest on August 6, 1939. Watson was the sole finisher in the annual race that year because of unusually rough water. The course record was about 3 hours and 40 minutes. Such races were popular on Great Salt Lake in the 1920s and 1930s. (Courtesy of Utah State Historical Society.)

Duck hunters pose with trophies from the Bear River Migratory Bird Refuge, probably in the late 1920s or early 1930s. The sanctuary, west of Brigham City, was created in 1928 and includes 80,000 acres of marsh, mudflats, and open water in wetlands where the Bear River enters the northeast arm of Great Salt Lake. (Courtesy of Utah State Historical Society.)

Driver Teddy Tetzlaff set a world land speed record of over 142 miles per hour on the Bonneville Salt Flats on August 14, 1914. The world-famous salt flats, a relic of Great Salt Lake's prehistoric predecessor, Lake Bonneville, cover some 150 square miles. The area used as a test track is near the twin towns of Wendover, Utah, and West Wendover, Nevada. (Courtesy of Utah State Historical Society.)

The race car *Mormon Meteor*, driven by David Abbott "Ab" Jenkins, streaks across the salt-white Bonneville Speedway in the 1930s. Jenkins drove the modified Duesenberg at 171 miles per hour in 1939 and also broke all 12-hour endurance records. Later, *Mormon Meteor III* set a 24-hour speed record of 161.180 miles per hour that was not broken until 1990. During the 1940s, Jenkins was mayor of Salt Lake City. (Courtesy of Utah State Historical Society.)

David Abbott "Ab" Jenkins poses with his *Mormon Meteor* racing team on September 20, 1937, at the Bonneville Salt Flats. This original *Meteor* set a 24-hour speed record, while in 1940, *Mormon Meteor III* established 21 different speed records at Bonneville. (Courtesy of Utah State Historical Society.)

The *Bluebird* rocketed to 304 miles per hour across the Bonneville Speedway on September 3, 1935, setting a world land speed record. The vehicle was driven by Sir Malcolm Campbell of England. All of his race cars were painted blue and named *Bluebird*. After Campbell retired, his son Donald continued the family's racing legacy. (Courtesy of Utah State Historical Society.)

Five

"FLOAT LIKE A CORK" RESORTS

Early Utahns found themselves avidly attracted to Great Salt Lake, where bathers could "float like a cork." About 10 accommodations sprouted by the late 1800s. None survive today as formal resorts at their original locations.

Lake Side, which opened for business in June 1870, was located southwest of Kaysville. By the 1882, season it was providing some 30,000 "baths" annually.

Lake Point was also founded 1870, on the south shore. By 1874, it had a dining hall and dancing room, plus 40 hotel rooms. It fell victim to the popularity of its rivals by 1890.

Garfield Beach, southwest of Black Rock, began attracting patrons in 1875. It was described as "Utah's great sanitarium resort." A fire destroyed it in 1904.

The first Black Rock opened in 1876 but did not catch on. It soon fell into disrepair but had several revivals over the decades

Lake Shore, described as a modest resort, opened in 1879 in southwest Farmington. It closed by 1890.

Lake Park started on July 15, 1886, between Lake Side and Lake Shore in west Farmington. By 1895, the resort was impacted by low water levels, so the operation moved inland to a pond in 1896. It evolved into today's Lagoon amusement park.

Syracuse Resort opened on July 4, 1887, when 13 train cars brought 2,000 people there for a swim. A train line from Ogden extended to the 93-acre resort, described as "an oasis in the desert." Built where today's Antelope Island causeway begins, it closed in 1892.

Saltair, the lake's legendary resort, was also the most elegant and popular. It opened on Memorial Day 1893. Built as an ornate pavilion over the south shore on 2,500 wooden pilings, it originally had 1,000 bathhouses. Fires destroyed it in both 1925 and 1970. Though swamped by floods during the 1980s, a third incarnation still exists nearby as a concert venue.

Sunset Beach was another southern resort, located 20 miles west of Salt Lake City, that began in about 1938. It hung on, despite Saltair's popularity, until about 1968, when ambitious expansion plans failed.

Albert Charles Tissandier, a French illustrator, architect, aviator, and editor, visited the United States in the 1880s and created a set of detailed drawings on Great Salt Lake's south shore during a stop in Utah. This example shows water lapping at Black Rock. (Albert Charles Tissandier, French, View of Great Salt Lake, 1885, pencil and paper. From the Permanent Collection of the Utah Museum of Fine Arts.)

In this detailed drawing from the 1880s, French illustrator Albert Charles Tissandier captured an early commercial establishment—a bathing house, dining hall, and pier—on Great Salt Lake. (Albert Charles Tissandier, French, *Bathing Establishment on the Salt Lake*, 1885, pencil and paper. From the Permanent Collection of the Utah Museum of Fine Arts.)

The Garfield Beach bathing resort, which opened in 1875, was located about a mile and a half east of Lake Point on Great Salt Lake's south shore. The handsome structure's claim to fame was its 165-foot-by-62-foot dance pavilion over the lake. (Courtesy of the Church of Jesus Christ of Latter-day Saints.)

Utah Western Railway's extension into Tooele County provided convenient public access to Garfield Beach resort, as illustrated in this 1880 stereograph image. The Black Rock formation rises from the lake in the background. Railroads simplified travel to several south beach resorts, which were west of Salt Lake City. On average, six trains a day rolled to Garfield. (Courtesy of the Church of Jesus Christ of Latter-day Saints.)

Garfield Beach resort was in its heyday when Salt Lake photographer C.R. Savage composed this undated image. The pavilion was packed, and Great Salt Lake's near-shore waters were dotted with bathers. Some 80,000 visitors flocked to the $70,000 resort in 1888. Garfield lost popularity when Saltair resort opened in 1893. The pavilion was destroyed by fire in 1904. (Courtesy of the Church of Jesus Christ of Latter-day Saints.)

Copyright 1897 by T. D. Rust

This 1897 photograph by T.D. Rust captures a quieter view of Garfield Beach resort's promenade and pavilion, four years after rival Saltair opened nearby. The then-dwindling Great Salt Lake had also reduced the depth of the water around the Garfield resort. Saltair was constructed farther out in the lake. (Courtesy of Library of Congress.)

This is a rare view of Garfield Beach Resort, probably in the late 1880s, looking northeast. The Black Rock formation is in the middle of the photograph. (Courtesy of the Church of Jesus Christ of Latter-day Saints.)

An 1875 photograph features Clinton's Hotel, also sometimes known as "Lake Point," at the lake's south end. The steamer *Garfield* is shown docked in the picture. The resort was built by Dr. Jeter Clinton in 1870 and had a dining hall, a dancing room, and 40 hotel rooms. It likely closed by 1890, a victim of Saltair's popularity. (Courtesy of the Church of Jesus Christ of Latter-day Saints.)

"Bathing at Garfield Beach" is the title of this undated photograph by C.R. Savage. It is probably from the late 1880s. Note Black Rock in the background, as well as the "Boats for rent" sign hanging from the building. None of the bathers shown here appear to be in water deeper than their waist. (Courtesy of the Church of Jesus Christ of Latter-day Saints.)

A couple poses in the dark recesses of Giant's Cave in this 1905 stereograph. The cavern, above Garfield Beach, was the larger of two caves on the mountainside. Giant's Cave was described as being 500 feet in length, with a varied clearance of 10 feet or more. It was highly publicized in Salt Lake newspapers starting in 1884. (Courtesy of Library of Congress.)

Fully attired bathers swim and float in the dense waters of Great Salt Lake, near the old Black Rock resort in 1904. The resort opened in 1876 but closed in the mid-1890s. The lake, though, remained accessible, and other beach enterprises were attempted there through the first half of the 20th century. (Courtesy of Library of Congress.)

"Floating like a cork" was a popular summer pastime for northern Utahns and visitors around the turn of the 20th century, as illustrated in this 1904 stereograph scene at the south shore's Black Rock in 1904. The resorts at this location ebbed and flowed with fashion, the economy, and Great Salt Lake's fickle shorelines. (Courtesy of Library of Congress.)

Perched on a boulder, a man enjoys the solitude and view at Great Salt Lake's Black Rock in about the year 1910. A portion of Stansbury Island is visible northwest to the right, and the Stansbury Mountains are in the distance to the left. Black Rock itself is believed to have tumbled from nearby Oquirrh Mountain slopes during the time of Lake Bonneville. (Courtesy of Utah State Historical Society.)

Saltair's fanciful multi-domed pavilion fills the background of this 1897 stereographic view by St. Louis–based photographer B.L. Tingley. Saltair had been built, at a cost of about $250,000, four years earlier on Great Salt Lake's south shore by the Church of Jesus Christ of Latter-day Saints and partners. The church hoped it would be a relaxing, family-oriented establishment. (Courtesy of the Library of Congress.)

Saltair's turreted pavilion rises like a royal palace above Great Salt Lake in a 1901 photograph. Located about 16 miles from downtown Salt Lake City, the resort was long the most popular such resort. It was intended to be a "Coney Island of the West." The Moorish design was by Richard K.A. Kletting, also architect of the Utah State Capitol. (Courtesy of the Library of Congress.)

"Try to sink" was perhaps the most popular slogan at Saltair resort, thanks to the Great Salt Lake's salt content of 25 percent or so. In decades like this one, possibly around 1920, the lake level was high, and swimming opportunities encircled the fancy resort. (Courtesy of Utah State Historical Society.)

This is an unusual view from the rear of Saltair in the early 1920s. The resort's first major fire occurred on April 22, 1925, not long after the image was made. Saltair was quickly rebuilt, bigger and better than ever. The Great Depression, which began in 1929, proved more challenging to the lakeside resort than any fire. (Courtesy of Utah State Historical Society.)

Saltair's pavilion looms in the background as, script on this 1902 Johnson Company "stereoscopic view" observes, "Everybody has fun in the Great Salt Lake." Saltair expanded its offerings in subsequent years. In 1909, the resort added a floating two-story café, called Leviathan, alongside the pier. The resort also boasted what it billed as the world's largest dance floor inside its pavilion. (Courtesy of the Library of Congress.)

Saltair's Great Pavilion, with winged side piers, was built away from the beach, allowing ample water depth in the resort's early years, as Great Salt Lake's shore intermittently receded and returned. (Courtesy of the Library of Congress.)

A rail spur rolled passengers to Saltair, about 16 miles distant from Salt Lake City. The Church of Jesus Christ of Latter-day Saints built Saltair as an all-American attraction but, apparently, found it difficult to maintain the desired family-friendly atmosphere. The resort was sold to a group of church members and investors in 1906, in part because beer was being sold there. (Courtesy of Utah State Historical Society.)

Some Saltair patrons, as demonstrated by the women in this undated stereograph card, were happy to float around Great Salt Lake's shallow off-shore water inside a small boat. Saltair was at its peak in the 1920s, when it boasted about half-a-million visitors a year. (Courtesy of the Library of Congress.)

"Fun for all in the Great Salt Lake" is highlighted in this 1902 photograph. The modest yet fashionable swim suits of the early 1900s often covered both women and men from shoulder to ankle, as illustrated in this picture. Big-brimmed hats undoubtedly offered protection from the sun and glare in an era before sunscreen lotions were available. (Courtesy of the Library of Congress.)

You see JOHNSON all over the world.

Bathers of all ages pose for a camera at Saltair—an extended family, perhaps? The 1902 stereograph only notes that it portrays "A jolly party in the Great Salt Lake." Saltair opened on Memorial Day in 1893 with 11,000 patrons. It was by far the most popular Great Salt Lake resort. Saltair was world famous and simply a must-visit in days of yore. (Courtesy of the Library of Congress.)

A stereoview card from 1904 pictures a gentleman strolling the pier in front of Saltair's "Great Pavilion" at a quiet hour. Stereoviews, or stereographs, were most popular from 1860 to 1920. They featured paired images of popular locations, such as vacation spots, as well as artworks, architecture, and scenic wonders. These were placed in an instrument called a stereoscope, which produced a three-dimensional effect for viewers. (Courtesy of Library of Congress.)

The Saltair Pavilion's cavernous interior was captured by Salt Lake City photographer C.R. Savage around 1900. Saltair was a popular venue for concerts, dances, boxing matches, political gatherings, and more. The original pavilion was destroyed by fire in April 1925. (Courtesy of the Church of Jesus Christ of Latter-day Saints.)

The Church of Jesus Christ of Latter-day Saints not only built Saltair but added a train line linking Great Salt Lake's south shore to Salt Lake City. As hinted in this photograph, from about 1900 the engines and cars rolled up a pier to the pavilion. Roundtrip fares to Saltair began at 25¢ in the 1890s but rose to 35¢ by 1910. (Courtesy of the Church of Jesus Christ of Latter-day Saints.)

The entire Saltair complex was captured in this undated aerial perspective, probably in the 1950s. Note the resort's wooden roller coaster and that the lake's waters have receded from Saltair. At one time, the resort boasted a Ferris wheel, a merry-go-round, and various midway games. It even hosted bicycle races, rodeos, boat rides, fireworks, and hot-air balloon trips. (Courtesy of Utah State Historical Society.)

Saltair's 1925 fire ravaged its 110-foot-high wooden roller coaster, the "Giant Racer." As with the resort's pavilion, the coaster went through various iterations and burned a couple of times. The final variation was blown down during a 1957 windstorm and never rebuilt. Saltair had other accidents, mishaps, and disasters over the decades, including drownings, collapsed stairways, and other fierce winds. (Courtesy of the Church of Jesus Christ of Latter-day Saints.)

Saltair was sporadically plagued by fires. This contact print, with three images from a 1967 blaze, was taken by a *Salt Lake Tribune* photographer. The resort's closed pavilion was spared on this occasion, but in 1970, this fabled incarnation burned to the ground. (Courtesy of Utah State Historical Society.)

Great Salt Lake and Saltair's shuttered pavilion, posing as a spooky, abandoned carnival, were featured in the 1962 horror film *Carnival of Souls*. Actress Candace Hilligoss starred as a woman tormented by visions after a car accident. In one scene, ghouls swirl on Saltair's once famous dance floor. Saltair was lost to fire in 1970, and in a way, the film preserves its memory. (Herts-Lion International Corporation/ Public Domain.)

Lake Park, located on the lake's east shore, opened in 1886. It was built by Simon Bamberger, later Utah's governor from 1917 to 1921. When the resort was relocated next to a Farmington pond, his open-air dancing pavilion was the only feature moved east in 1896. There, it became an amusement park called Lagoon, which still thrives. The pavilion was dismantled in 2004. (Courtesy of the Church of Jesus Christ of Latter-day Saints.)

This is a rare photograph of the bathhouses and bathing area at Farmington's Lake Park resort, probably in about 1890. The receding Great Salt Lake in the early 1890s forced the resort to move inland after the 1895 season. (Courtesy of the Church of Jesus Christ of Latter-day Saints.)

A photograph, probably from the late 1880s, records Lake Park resort in west Farmington. The resort was primarily built to increase passenger traffic on the urban railroad, hence the engine prominently on display in this picture. Also, note the tents in the picture, which were used as lodging in the resort's earliest years. (Courtesy of the Church of Jesus Christ of Latter-day Saints.)

Only a few photographs like this exist of bathers and the water at west Farmington's Lake Park, which only lasted for about nine years, from 1886 until 1895. By 1896, the resort had relocated inland because of a shrinking Great Salt Lake and became Lagoon. (Courtesy of the Church of Jesus Christ of Latter-day Saints.)

The Syracuse Bathing Resort opened on July 4, 1887, when 13 train cars transported some 2,000 patrons there. It was located just north of today's Antelope Drive, near where the Davis County Causeway to Antelope Island State Park begins. Described as "an oasis in the desert," it had 70 bathhouses and offered boat excursions to nearby islands. (Courtesy of Utah State Historical Society.)

VIEW AT SYRACUSE BATHING RESORT.

The Syracuse Bathing Resort boasted a grove of transplanted trees, hauled to the shore from Weber Canyon, in the nearby Wasatch Mountains. Although a train line offered convenient access to the 93-acre resort, the last transport of the night is said to have departed early at times, leaving visitors stranded overnight. The resort closed in 1892 after a six-season run. (Courtesy of Utah State Historical Society.)

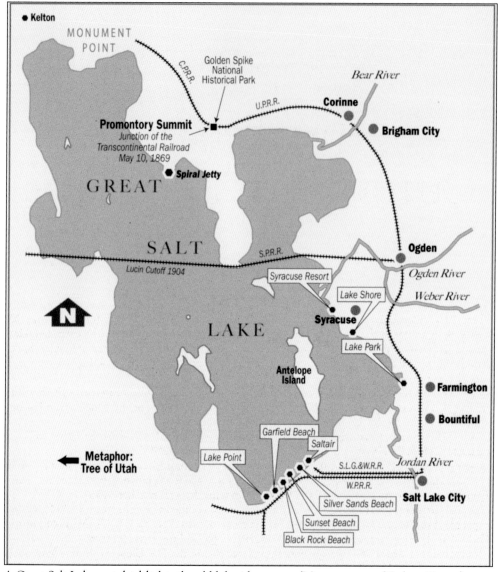

A Great Salt Lake map highlights the old lakeside resorts. (Map courtesy of Robert Noyce.)

Six

Golden Spike, the Cutoff, and Railroads

When the Golden Spike was ceremoniously driven at Utah's Promontory Summit on May 10, 1869, linking routes of the rival Central Pacific and Union Pacific Railroads, the event heralded a new era of transcontinental transportation. The achievement, commemorated at Golden Spike National Historical Park, has been described as the 19th century's equivalent of the 20th century's space flights to the moon.

However, it was apparent within a few decades that the serpentine route through the hills and passes north of Great Salt Lake created one of the most expensive and time-consuming rail bottlenecks in the nation. Something had to be done.

In 1902, the Southern Pacific Railroad system, a successor to the Central Pacific, began work on the Lucin Cutoff. The revolutionary bypass was to be part earthen-fill causeway and part trestle, spanning 25 miles of Great Salt Lake water and mudflat. When finished in 1904, the new 102-mile route between Ogden and Lucin, a water stop west of the lake that gave the cutoff its name, sliced almost 50 miles off most passenger and freight train trips through northern Utah.

Though efficient, the cutoff had its dangers. Two trains collided along the trestle in 1904, killing 26 people. But the most famous accident on the route occurred on New Year's Eve 1944, during World War II, when two trains collided, killing 48 people and injuring 79 others.

Today, a dirt-and-rock causeway has entirely replaced the trestle. The valuable century-old wooden beams were salvaged for resale.

However, construction of the causeway controversially split Great Salt Lake into two parts. The northern section, Gunnison Bay, receives little fresh water and has therefore become extremely dense and salty. It is often tinted purple to pink, due to salt-loving algae and bacteria. The southern section, Gilbert Bay in the lake's center, has better circulation, more freshwater tributaries, and supports a healthier ecosystem.

A bridge, completed in 2016, is expected to improve exchanges between the two bays over time, but the colorful divide continues to be highly visible from above—especially to satellite cameras and astronauts.

The driving of the first Transcontinental Railroad's last "Golden Spike" occurred on May 10, 1869, at Promontory Summit, Utah, just north of Great Salt Lake. Civil War photographer Andrew J. Russell took this photograph, celebrating the joining of the east and west tracks of the rival Union Pacific and Central Pacific Railroads. The original 17.6-karat spike is displayed at Stanford University. (Courtesy of Yale University Libraries.)

The momentous 1869 ceremony is regularly replicated at the Golden Spike National Historical Park, as it was during this event on May 10, 1956, as recorded by a *Salt Lake Tribune* photographer. The location, now part of the National Park Service, features a museum, auto tour routes, and replicas of the train engines, Union Pacific's No. 119 and Central Pacific's *Jupiter*, or No. 60. (Courtesy Utah State Historical Society.)

Utah Western Railway | *Looking west*
Great Salt Lake to right
Oquirrh Range to left, Onaqui Range in distance

This is the Western Pacific Railroad line in 1875. The route followed the south shore of Great Salt Lake, providing access to such sites as the Garfield Beach resort. The Oquirrh Mountains abruptly terminate south of the rail line. Great Salt Lake was near one of its highest water levels ever in 1875. (Courtesy of the Church of Jesus Christ of Latter-day Saints.)

A crew lays rails during construction of Lucin Cutoff at the turn of the 20th century. Rails of the Central Pacific Railroad, built east from California, and those of the Union Pacific, laid westward out of Omaha, Nebraska, met at Utah's Promontory Summit in 1869. From 1902 to 1904, Southern Pacific, which succeeded Central Pacific, built an almost straight causeway and trestle route across the lake. (Courtesy Utah State Historical Society.)

Supervisors in a boat oversee the driving of the last pile in the wooden railroad trestle system across Great Salt Lake on October 26, 1903. The mushy lake bed at times swallowed up Paul Bunyan–size posts and 20-ton rocks during construction of the Lucin Cutoff. The cross-lake route eliminated daunting railroad grades and curves over summits and terraces, saving the railroads time and money. (Courtesy Utah State Historical Society.)

Railroad officials and guests pose for a photograph celebrating completion of the Lucin Cutoff on Thanksgiving Day, November 26, 1903. On the extreme right, first row, is Edward Henry Harriman, president of the combined Southern Pacific Railroad-Union Pacific Railroad system. Freight trains started using the bypass in March 1904, and passenger trains started the following September. (Courtesy Utah State Historical Society.)

A Southern Pacific train rumbles across the Lucin Cutoff in 1905. The rail shortcut erased 44 miles from most freight and passenger train trips through northern Utah. The artery was hailed as the longest, straightest, most-level stretch of track ever built. The cutoff was named after the water stop and worker village of Lucin, west of Great Salt Lake. (Courtesy Utah State Historical Society.)

This is the Promontory Point railroad station, partway along the Lucin Cutoff, as it appeared in 1920. The location is at the southern end of Utah's Promontory Mountains and is not to be confused with Promontory Summit. Maintenance of the cutoff proved a challenge. Billowing salt water whitewashed workers and damaged machines, and pilings and earthworks settled into the lake bed's soft mud, requiring remedial repairs. (Courtesy Utah State Historical Society.)

Passengers and rescue crews gather along Lucin Cutoff tracks on January 1, 1945, after the route's worst disaster–Two trains collided on New Year's Eve 1944. The crash, at the height of rail traffic during World War II, killed 48 people and injured 79 others. The tragedy was not the cutoff's only major crash. Two trains also collided on February 19, 1904, killing 26 people. (Courtesy Utah State Historical Society.)

Survey crews in 1959 work along a new earthen causeway on the Lucin Cutoff, just before rails were to be set in place. The redesigned route ran mostly parallel to the old wooden trestle, which was aging and considered rickety. Some trains crawled along at 15 miles per house because of the trestle's sway, especially during storms. (Courtesy Utah State Historical Society.)

A 1971 photograph shows the junction where a new rock causeway, on the right, diverged from Lucin Cutoff's original, straight-line causeway and trestle section, left. Later, a period of high precipitation in northern Utah during the mid-1980s forced the railroad to dump trainloads of rock along the tracks to protect the route from record-high Great Salt Lake water levels. (Courtesy of Library of Congress.)

An aerial photograph from 1971 shows the original Lucin Cutoff on the left and a then-new earthen causeway section to the right. The causeways cut Great Salt Lake in two, isolating bays north and south. In 2016, a 300-foot-long trestle was installed to help water better circulate between saltier Gunnison Bay, to the north, and central Gilbert Bay, which receives more fresh water from tributaries. (Courtesy of Library of Congress.)

A bird's-eye view highlights Lucin Cutoff's original wooden trestle section. More than 38,000 trees were required to build this engineering marvel of its day. Another two million board feet of redwood were laid as planking. The huge project took 18 months to construct, requiring some 3,000 laborers, and cost more than $8 million—equivalent to about $230 million today. (Courtesy of Library of Congress.)

A photograph taken in 1971 from a choppy Great Salt Lake offers a perspective of the wooden Lucin Cutoff trestle's herculean pilings, posts, braces, caps, and bolts. The support piles were mostly Oregon fir, but other timber products were used as well. As historians say, the cutoff required a virtual "forest of trees." Great trainloads of timber chugged to Utah from all around the country. (Courtesy of Library of Congress.)

This 1971 view of the Lucin Cutoff shows its double track and service road. Almost three dozen trains a day traversed the route in the 1960s. By the early 21st century, traffic was down to about six freight trains a day in each direction. Most passenger trains now go through Salt Lake City, not Ogden, and follow the lake's south side, avoiding the cutoff. (Courtesy of Library of Congress.)

College students study the Lucin Cutoff in 1971 at a section where a wooden trestle meets the earth-and-rock fill causeway. The wooden trestle was vulnerable to fire. A blaze in November 1957 destroyed a section 600 feet long. Speed limits varied on the differing structures, like trains traversing Great Salt Lake traveled more slowly on the trestles than they did on the causeway portions. (Courtesy of Library of Congress.)

This 1971 photograph depicts the aging Lucin Cutoff trestle in the foreground and the causeway that replaced it in the background. In 1993, salvage companies began to reclaim all of the wood—some 20 million board feet—from the original trestle. By the year 2000, the century-old trestle had vanished, but its wood lives on as flooring, siding, cabinets, mantels, and such. (Courtesy of Library of Congress.)

A Union Pacific locomotive pulls a train across the Lucin Cutoff's trestle in an undated photograph. Since the wood section was only used on a limited basis after 1960, and not employed after about 1975, this picture is likely from the late 1950s. Trains also proceeded at a slower clip on this trestle in its later years for it had deteriorated and begun to sway. (Courtesy Utah State Historical Society.)

Seven

SALT, MINERALS, AND INDUSTRY

As John C. Fremont and his troop headed north in 1843 to the Oregon Trail after their first encounters with Great Salt Lake, the explorer observed that the area looked like prime territory for "a civilized settlement"—and that the big lake itself "will furnish exhaustless supplies of salt." Native Americans obtained salt from the lake before Fremont, and it has been harvested industrially since pioneers arrived, as have many other minerals. One estimate posits that Great Salt Lake harbors minerals worth more than $90 billion.

Various attempts have been made to stock the lake with such sea life as eels, oysters, and crabs. None of these succeeded. Neither saltwater nor freshwater fish, or most other creatures, can survive in the saline waters, which range from about 14-percent salt in Great Salt Lake's southern bays to 25 percent or more farther north. Only brine shrimp, brine flies, and certain algae and bacteria tolerate the lake's high salt content.

Today, mineral extraction is big business. By the late 19th century, Utah had several producers of sodium chloride, or common salt. Modern extractors develop vast evaporation ponds, which create patches of color when viewed from above. Besides table salt, they produce salt products for animals and for winter roadway use. Other products include sodium sulfate, used in paper and glass making; potassium sulfate for fertilizer; chlorine gas; and magnesium.

Oil companies, too, have been curious about what lies beneath. Natural oil or tar seeps bubble out of the lake bed off Rozel Point, near artist Robert Smithson's *Spiral Jetty*. Both the artwork site and sticky seeps are leased from the state.

The lake's only aquatic lifeforms are the brine shrimp. Each adult shrimp's almost-transparent body is less than a half inch long. Millions of birds feast on them, and the tiny crustaceans are also harvested to be used as fish food in aquariums.

Some people may recall ads toward the backs of comic books that sold "sea monkey" eggs, with fanciful drawings that made emergent creatures look rather simian—or human. These, believe it or not, are brine shrimp.

An antique photograph, perhaps from the turn of the 20th century, records a crew harvesting salt from Great Salt Lake's south shore. The Oquirrh Range's north end is in the background. Early settlers enjoyed outings to the lake and bathing in its hyper-saline water but also recognized that they were not going to have a problem acquiring salt for their daily needs. (Courtesy of the Church of Jesus Christ of Latter-day Saints.)

Another early photograph shows salt mining beside Great Salt Lake through an evaporation process. In the 19th century, harvesters employed the time-consuming method of boiling lake water for table salt and other uses but, later, created ponds that let the sun do the evaporative work on a greater scale. (Courtesy of Library of Congress.)

This postcard, probably from the early 1900s, highlights salt evaporation ponds and salt harvesting on the south shore of the Great Salt Lake. Note the railroad line amid the evaporation ponds, making transporting harvested salt much easier. (Courtesy of Boston Public Library.)

A 1918 photograph shows an unnamed saltworks factory, caked with the mineral. In August 1847, less than a month after the Mormon pioneers arrived in the Salt Lake Valley, a committee was created to obtain salt. The first haul, four days later, totaled 125 bushels of salt. It was, one pioneer observed, "as white as the Liverpool salt and just as fine." (Courtesy of Library of Congress.)

An early aerial photograph, taken from an airplane from Langley Air Force Base, Virginia, on December 26, 1929, pinpoints a circular saltworks operation in the desert west of Great Salt Lake. Once these salt flats dried out during the warmer months of the year, they were very accessible. Great Salt Lake is believed to contain an estimated 4.5 billion tons of salt. (Courtesy of Library of Congress.)

An ore smelting plant was photographed in 1925 from an airplane by US Army captain A.W. Stevens. Utah Copper Company, today part of Rio Tinto's Kennecott Copper operations, established the first open-pit copper mine in the United States at Bingham Canyon, and transported ore for processing to Garfield, near Magna, between the Oquirrh Mountains and the south edge of Great Salt Lake. (Courtesy of Library of Congress.)

Utah's Royal Crystal salt plant, as it appeared in 1950, was in Tooele County, north of Grantsville and not far from the southwest edge of Great Salt Lake, near the source of its salt. The plant had direct railroad access, and the firm was one of the original salt-mining companies in northern Utah. (Courtesy of Utah State Historical Society.)

A Royal Crystal Salt Company worker drives a tractor churning salt on March 9, 1950, in Tooele County. The salt accumulated in a diked evaporation pond beside Great Salt Lake, where the sun did much of the work. Other early harvesting enterprises included Jeremy Salt Company, Intermountain Salt Company, and Inland Salt Company. They have been succeeded by Morton Salt and other operations. (Courtesy of Utah State Historical Society.)

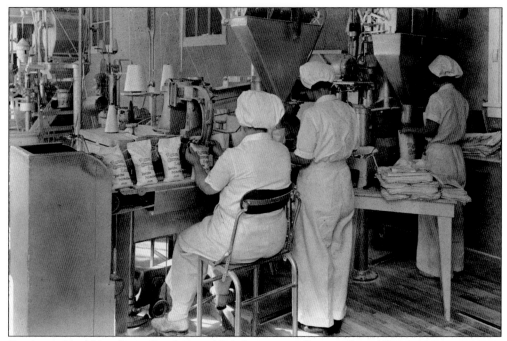

Employees bag table salt in a Royal Crystal Salt factory near Grantsville in 1950. A Montana mining boom in the 1860s spurred development of commercial salt mining around Great Salt Lake. Large amounts of sodium chloride were needed to convert silver in ore to silver chloride, which could then be further refined. Today, salt is destined for cattle ranges, snowy highways, and dinner tables. (Courtesy of Utah State Historical Society.)

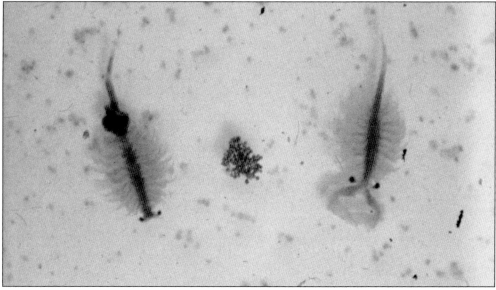

Tiny brine shrimp thrive in vast numbers in Great Salt Lake. Other aquatic lifeforms, except certain algae and bacteria, cannot tolerate the lake's salinity like they do. The shrimp produce larvae, or eggs, that are harvested as food for fish farms and commercial shrimp operations. The brine shrimp are also a vital food resource for about 10 million migratory birds, representing some 250 species. (Courtesy of Antelope Island State Park.)

Several companies use specialized harvester boats, containment devices, and vacuum pumps to glean cloudy streaks of brine shrimp and their eggs, one of the few lifeforms in Great Salt Lake, as depicted in this slide photograph, from the mid-20th century. The tiny crustaceans consume the lake's algae, and in turn, they are eaten by birds and are harvested as food for fish and shrimp farms. (Courtesy of Antelope Island State Park.)

An Amoco Corporation drilling rig floats into place in Great Salt Lake in June 1978. Amoco leased 620,000 acres from the state to search for oil, primarily under the lake. The company drilled 15 marine wells but stopped work in January 1981 because of high costs. The Utah Geological Survey says oil production began around the turn of the 20th century, with minor success. (Courtesy of Utah State Historical Society.)

Sitting at the bottom of a closed drainage called the Great Basin, the terminal Great Salt Lake accumulates from its tributary rivers vast quantities of dissolved minerals and salts, which are the focus of multimillion-dollar extraction industries. Artful heaps of salt, harvested from solar and crystallizing ponds, rise at a Morton Salt operation in this 1962 image, taken by a *Salt Lake Tribune* photographer. (Courtesy of Utah State Historical Society.)

One of many operations on Great Salt Lake, today's Morton Salt Company plant in Utah is near Stansbury Island. Morton is noted for its familiar symbol featuring a little girl with an umbrella, a spilling salt container, and the century-old anti-clumping slogan, "When it rains, it pours." The firm processes and distributes common table salt, as well as grades suitable for livestock, water-softeners, and winter deicing. (Ray Boren photograph.)

Eight

THE RISING AND FALLING LAKE

If there is something Great Salt Lake does well, it is fluctuating. Inconstancy is the inland sea's constant.

The lake's annual average surface elevation has been about 4,196 feet above sea level since the US Geological Survey began monitoring it in 1875. In the mid-1960s, the lake's level hit the lowest recorded to that time, 4,191.35. By the mid-1980s, it had rebounded to a record high elevation of 4,211.6, covering 3,300 square miles of surface area. More recently, the level has again dropped to record lows—an inch below the 1960s mark by 2022—abetted by drought, a drying climate, and continuing diversion of its tributaries. Wildlife is endangered. Toxic dust storms and pollution are feared. Utahns worry.

These fluctuations are not without precedent. The lake is, after all, the climatically challenged descendant of humongous, and much deeper, Lake Bonneville. And Great Salt Lake's obituary has been written several times.

"America's famous 'Dead Sea' soon to be dry land" was, for instance, a 1924 headline in the *Ogden Standard-Examiner*. The story predicted the lake would vanish entirely, laying bare "one of the richest mineral deposits on earth." Similar death-knells would sound in the 1960s, and are doing so again. "Race is on to save Great Salt Lake: Will it be enough?" a headline wondered atop a national Associated Press story in 2022.

The news reports were just the opposite in the 1980s. From a low point in the mid-1960s, the lake level rose 20 feet in just two decades, thanks to several wet years. Great Salt Lake eroded portions of Interstate 80 on the lake's south end, inundated farmland, flooded Saltair and other enterprises, and washed out the causeway to Antelope Island.

To divert some of the incoming water, the state of Utah installed three giant pumps on the lake's west side. They were designed to move water, via a short canal, into the Newfoundland Basin. The flood threat abated. The pumps, no longer in use, are maintained should they be required again—which does not look to be any time soon.

The massive pumps on Great Salt Lake's west side are under construction in this c. 1986 image. Considered an emergency project due to flooding around the lake, the pumping station was operational in only nine-and-a-half months. The pumps sent water into a four-mile-long canal and into the western Newfoundland Basin. The state spends about $10,000 a year to keep the pumps ready. (Courtesy of Wally Gwynn, Utah Geological Survey.)

Great Salt Lake flooding, which endangered infrastructure and enterprises in the 1980s, prompted Utah to invest $60 million in a set of pumps designed to move excess water west into Newfoundland Basin. Here, on April 10, 1987, VIPs watch as the pumps are first switched on. The pumps ran for about 28 months, until June 1989. They lowered the lake by 18 inches. (Courtesy of Wally Gwynn, Utah Geological Survey.)

Flooding in 1984 near Great Salt Lake threatened highways, causeways, and railroads and inundated the most recent site of Saltair. The pavilion, which opened in 1982, flooded as the lake hit its highest level ever, putting the main floor under five feet of water. By June 1993, the lake had receded, and Saltair re-opened as a concert venue—on the original resort's centennial. (Courtesy of Utah Geological Survey.)

Coauthor Lynn Arave stands atop a portion of the washed-out, formerly paved causeway to Antelope Island in April 1991. The rising Great Salt Lake eroded large portions of the road in 1983. Storms had previously damaged sections of the causeway in the 1970s. In the mid-1990s, the roadbed was raised, and as Great Salt Lake is shrinking, there have been no washouts since. (Roger Arave photograph.)

Young Taylor Arave stands in Fremont Island's bone-dry Wenner Bay in September 2008. His raised hiking pole approaches how high the waters of Great Salt Lake would have been there in 1986, when the lake reached a record 4,211.85 feet above sea level. The lake was some 17 feet lower than that in 2008, meaning Fremont was technically no longer an island. (Lynn Arave photograph.)

Three horses gallop freely along the dry edge of Fremont Island's Kit Carson Bay in September 2008. Since Great Salt Lake was shrinking, what had been under water from the late 1960s to about 2003 had become semipermanent dry ground. A natural sandbar, about seven miles long, connects Fremont with the causeway to Antelope Island. (Lynn Arave photograph.)

Taylor Arave examines sandy soil along a natural sandbar leading to Fremont Island in 2008. Great Salt Lake has fluctuated since Mormon pioneers settled the area in 1847. A graph of its elevation changes resembles a stock market chart. Since the late 1990s, the lake has been shrinking due to drought, a changing climate, and the diversion of tributary water for irrigation and other human purposes. (Lynn Arave photograph.)

Taylor Arave poses next to a landlocked buoy in front of Fremont Island in 2008. The buoy was placed there, probably in the 1990s, to warn of low and declining water levels ahead. What was left on the dry lake bed when the salty water was gone? A few old bottles here and there, occasional pockets of salt, or a tumbleweed, but otherwise just crusty sand. (Lynn Arave photograph.)

Metal gate posts rise from Great Salt Lake in a 1977 photograph. When the lake level was high, the two posts marked the start of the natural sandbar to Fremont Island. Once visible along the Davis County Causeway to Antelope Island, they were removed when the lake level dropped. A stone jetty subsequently marked the sandbar's beginning. (Lynn Arave photograph.)

This area west of Farmington is the eastern edge of Great Salt Lake when levels are higher. Indeed, a resort called Lake Park thrived here from 1886 to 1895. With the receding lake now about a mile away, it is simply brush and salty plain. Lake Park moved two miles inland in 1896 and became today's Lagoon amusement park. The Oquirrh Mountains are in the background. (Lynn Arave photograph.)

For much of modern history Black Rock has been a prominent islet on Great Salt Lake's south shore, lapped by saline waves. But in this 2012 photograph, the landmark, left high and dry by the receding lake, looks more like a small butte. Several resorts sprouted here. The north slopes of the Oquirrh Mountains rise in the background, as does Rio Tinto's 1,215-foot-tall Garfield copper smelter smokestack. (Ray Boren photograph.)

These three satellite photographs highlight Great Salt Lake's dramatic elevation changes over a 35-year span. (Courtesy Utah Division of Natural Resources.)

Erratic and declining water levels wreak havoc on the south shore's Great Salt Lake State Park and Marina. During extreme drought the marina looks much like a ghost town, as in this 2022 image. Most boats have been hoisted from the too-shallow water to sit mothballed onshore, awaiting better days, or are simply hauled away. A smaller harbor on Antelope Island is unusable at such times. (Ray Boren photograph.)

A *Salt Lake Tribune* staff member took this photograph, showing a US Air Force plane that crashed into Farmington Bay on Great Salt Lake's east side, in February 1954. A number of aircraft, boats, and even trains have crashed or sunk in the lake over the decades. A dozen Army Rangers and Air Force special operations airmen were killed in a 1992 helicopter crash. (Courtesy of Utah State Historical Society.)

Nine

GREAT SALT LAKE TODAY

Great Salt Lake may not be quite as "great" as it used to be, at least in size. Its shores seem to be fading from view. Yet the lake remains a valuable resource for the birds and other wildlife that rest, nest, range, and feed there; for its impact on Utah's economy; and certainly, for its strange beauty.

The smaller lake has exposed an additional 750 square miles of lake bed, leading to more dust storms. Scientists warn that Wasatch Front-bound squalls can be laden with particulates and potentially harmful toxins and pollutants. The lake also is still big enough to cause the so-called "lake effect," which can enhance the snowfall from winter storms. And periodically, there is also a "lake stink," a breeze-lifted odor that annoys visitors and nearby residents.

Great Salt Lake's open spaces, wildlife, and recreational opportunities, so near Utah's population centers, remain a boon to those ready to explore. Though subject to the rising and falling lake, *Spiral Jetty*, the late artist Robert Smithson's landscape masterwork, is more popular than ever, attracting visitors from around the world to remote Rozel Point. Antelope Island State Park is hailed by commentators as one of the best in the country and as an excellent place to experience Great Salt Lake.

Utahns and observers from around the world are better informed about Great Salt Lake's importance as both an ecosystem and a resource. Strides have been made to curb unfettered pollution. In 2010, the Utah Legislature created the Great Salt Lake Advisory Council to counsel lawmakers, state agencies, and local communities about ways to help the lake, and to keep it from drying up entirely. It has recommended strategies to promote change, including helping more water actually reach the lake. In January 2022, the state also held a Great Salt Lake Summit to consider ways to revitalize the lake and to address long-term problems.

House Speaker Brad Wilson said the following at the summit: "The Great Salt Lake isn't just the name of our capital city or the name of a lake. It's absolutely part of the identity as to who we are as Utahns."

NASA astronauts catch fascinating views of Great Salt Lake and have been recording the changing lake levels for many years. This image from 2003 shows exposed lake bed, as well as patterned evaporative salt and mineral ponds on northeastern and southwestern bays. Due to drought, many of the lake's former islands are connected to the mainland. (Courtesy of the National Archives.)

This NASA photograph, a 2006 peek through apparatus of the International Space Station's Destiny module, looks down upon Great Salt Lake and other portions of northern Utah and southern Idaho, including Utah Lake at the bottom and Bear Lake to the upper right. (Courtesy of the National Archives.)

A view of Great Salt Lake, from high above and looking east, was taken in July 2011 from the Space Shuttle Atlantis. Despite a few puffy clouds, the slicing effect of the Lucin Cutoff railroad causeway is obvious. Communities dotting the lake's shores, from Brigham City on the left to Salt Lake City on the right, sit at the base of the Wasatch Mountains. (Courtesy of the National Archives.)

Lucin Cutoff, the railroad causeway, zigs and zags across Great Salt Lake in this 2009 aerial photograph. The section on the right is a newer earthen section, completed in the 1990s, which replaced an aging wooden trestle that allowed a straighter dash across the lake. (Ray Boren photograph.)

An F-16C Flying Falcon jet fighter, from the 419th Fighter Wing based at Utah's Hill Air Force Base, is photographed from another aircraft over Great Salt Lake during a training exercise in the late 1990s. The strip at the top of the picture is likely the Lucin Cutoff. (Courtesy of the National Archives.)

Armed with AIM-9 Sidewinder missiles, an F-16 jet fighter crosses the lake, headed for a training exercise over the West Desert range in 1987. The 419th Fighter Wing is part of the US Air Force Reserve. The rugged Lakeside Mountains are visible in the background. (Courtesy of the National Archives.)

Like panes of glass, evaporation ponds glitter on a portion of Great Salt Lake northeast of rocky-topped Fremont Island, in an aerial photograph from 2009. The Lucin Cutoff railroad causeway crosses at center beyond the ponds, with a short trestle opening on the right, allowing an exchange of lake waters. (Ray Boren photograph.)

Industrial ponds on Great Salt Lake use the sun's energy to evaporate water from the shallow brine, so that the dried salts and various minerals left behind can be harvested. In this 2009 aerial image, some of the ponds on the lake's northeast shore have been mechanically furrowed as part of the drying process. (Ray Boren photograph.)

Levees criss-cross portions of Great Salt Lake, separating mineral ponds, and allowing workers and industrial equipment access to them. The bordering dikes, angles, and colorful tints of various ponds create eye-pleasing designs that can resemble abstract art. (Ray Boren photograph.)

US Magnesium Corporation's plant is located on the west side of Great Salt Lake. Although it is in a remote location at Rowley, Utah, the plant, shown in a 2009 aerial, employs several hundred workers. The plant's previous owner/operator was often referred to as the nation's worst polluter in the 1980s and 1990s. Both the bankrupt predecessor and the present firm reached agreements to control hazardous substances. (Ray Boren photograph.)

Downtown Salt Lake City's skyline and the snow-blanketed Wasatch Mountains pop in this perspective from Antelope Island, taken on a wintry February day in 2012. Landscape artists such as Gilbert Munger, an Easterner fascinated with the American West, painted similar Great Salt Lake scenes in the 19th century. (Ray Boren photograph.)

Artist Gilbert Munger painted several Salt Lake area landscapes in the 1870s, including this striking view looking southeast from Great Salt Lake. His painting includes sailboats, flying waterfowl, small buildings, and such familiar Wasatch summits as Mount Olympus (the escarpment to the left). (Gilbert Davis Munger, American, *Great Salt Lake and The Wasatch*, ca. 1870s, oil on academy board. From the Permanent Collection of the Utah Museum of Fine Arts.)

Wetlands along Great Salt Lake shores are vital to migrating birds and other creatures. Among the refuges on the lake's east side is Farmington Bay Waterfowl Management Area, in the foreground here, as seen from the top of the Wasatch Mountains in 2020. Although streams make their way into the bay, drought has emptied the lake bed toward Antelope Island. Farther west is central, and deeper, Gilbert Bay. (Ray Boren photograph.)

The seven-mile-long Davis County Causeway links Antelope Island to the mainland, as shown in this 2009 photograph taken from the state park's visitor center. The island's marina, often unusable due to the lake's low levels, nestles to the left of the causeway. The cross-lake road's east side connects to Antelope Drive in Syracuse, which intersects with Interstate 15 and other major routes. (Ray Boren photograph.)

Antelope Island's summit, 6,596-foot Frary Peak, and other ridges are dusted with snow in this February 2016 photograph. The view is southeast from Buffalo Point, over White Rock Bay at Antelope Island State Park. Frary Peak, named for early homesteaders, is accessible by a 6.9-mile roundtrip hike. (Ray Boren photograph.)

A hiker stands atop Frary Peak, the highest point on Antelope Island, in this 2015 photograph. The view is southward, toward western Salt Lake County and the Oquirrh Mountains. Much of Antelope Island seems like a quiet national park, even though the populous Wasatch Front is less than 10 miles away. (Lynn Arave photograph.)

American bison—popularly known as buffalo—freely roam Antelope Island today. This 2015 photograph shows a few grazing near the roadway. Bison may have lived anciently on Antelope Island, but did not make a permanent home there. It was not until the early 1920s, when a silent movie, *The Covered Wagon*, was made, that bison (or buffalo) became a renowned part of the isle's animal population. (Ray Boren photograph.)

In this perspective looking east from Antelope Island on a cloudy winter day, the Wasatch Mountains reflect on calm Great Salt Lake waters. Antelope Island usually receives less snowfall than Wasatch Front. (Ray Boren photograph.)

Lines of wispy, wavy cirrus clouds stream over Great Salt Lake's Bridger Bay in this 2020 photograph. Fremont Island is in the distance, to the north, with peaks and slopes of the higher Promontory Range visible just beyond it. (Ray Boren photograph.)

Larry Saunders and Steve Hubbard inspect what is left of the Wenner family's stone house on Fremont Island in June 1982, after a seven-mile canoe trip there. Photographs taken of this 1880s house in the 1940s show it still had tall stone walls at that time. Storms and winds took their toll in the intervening four decades. Today, all that is left is a low foundation. (Lynn Arave photograph.)

A stone memorial and plaque mark the grave of Judge Uriah J. Wenner and Kate Wenner, as it appeared on Fremont Island in 2008. The couple and their children lived on the island in the late 19th century. Uriah died there of tuberculosis in 1891. Kate passed away 50 years later, and her ashes were interred with her late husband's. (Lynn Arave photograph.)

Frontiersman Kit Carson, while exploring Great Salt Lake with John C. Fremont, scratched a cross on a Fremont Island rock in 1843. This is how it looked in 2008. The cruciform mark, sketched on a gray stone face near the top of the isle's Castle Rock, has become a Catholic relic in Utah. It predates the 1847 arrival of Mormon pioneers. (Lynn Arave photograph.)

Site of a bustling beach and resort for more than a century—and the subject of countless photographs, illustrations, and postcards—Black Rock remains a highly visible, if often quiet, landmark near Saltair and beside Interstate 80. Vehicles have been able to approach it in recent years, and it is a destination via the Sunset Beach trail from Great Salt Lake State Park and Marina. (Ray Boren photograph.)

Blue herons perch high atop a rookery in Great Salt Lake–related wetlands in March 2016. Thousands of shore birds find suitable places to nest around the lake, but it does not hurt if humans occasionally lend a helping hand, as with these refuge towers. (Ray Boren photograph.)

Herons and other birds spend a frigid winter's day in January 2007 beside an open spot on an icy lagoon at the Farmington Bay Waterfowl Management Area. The refuge, west of the city of Farmington, is a breeding and feeding spot for many species of birds, from meadowlarks and various ducks to kestrels and eagles. Birdwatching is popular, and there is a hunting season for some species. (Ray Boren photograph.)

A flock of American white pelicans swoops over the Ogden Bay Waterfowl Management Area, in an aerial photograph taken from a plane flying above the birds. The wetlands are essentially a delta, fed by the Weber and Ogden Rivers, which provide about 14 percent of Great Salt Lake's incoming water. (Ray Boren photograph.)

Tundra swans, ducks, and other waterfowl flock to the US Fish and Wildlife Service's Bear River Migratory Bird Refuge, west of Brigham City, in this 2012 photograph. The refuge includes an education and visitor center off Interstate 15. A paved road continues west a dozen miles beside the Bear River to an unpaved 10-mile auto route along the refuge's levees and lagoons, frequented by millions of birds. (Ray Boren photograph.)

"Duckville," which was near today's entry to the lagoons of the Bear River Migratory Bird Refuge, west of Brigham City, historically has been a location of several hunting clubs and their lodges, as illustrated in this reflective 2016 image. The wetlands and refuge were inundated by floods and rising lake water, especially in the 1970s and 1980s, which damaged buildings and hurt the clubs operating them. (Ray Boren photograph.)

A gull snacks along a brine fly streak on an Antelope Island beach in 2021. Several species of gull frequent Great Salt Lake and northern Utah. Most common is the California gull, which is also (despite its name) Utah's state bird. The latter acclaim is because flocks of the birds devoured crickets feasting on settlers' fragile crops during the pioneer era, which was deemed a miracle. (Ray Boren photograph.)

Scoop up a handful of Great Salt Lake's light-colored sand, as in this 2021 photograph, and the curiously rounded nature of the individual grains is revealed. The grains are ooids, oolitic ovals that form as calcium carbonate coalesces in layers on tiny bits of minerals or other matter. "Ooid" and "oolitic" mean their shapes are egg-like. (Ray Boren photograph.)

114

The North Davis Sewer District plant is located on the edge of Farmington Bay and Great Salt Lake, near the causeway to Antelope Island. Until the early 1960s, raw sewage was commonly released into Great Salt Lake from the Wasatch Front. Today, all water is treated first. A new pipeline has been built to transport the North Davis water even farther, to the lake's central Gilbert Bay. (Lynn Arave photograph.)

This is how the area looks today where the Syracuse Bathing Resort was situated at the turn of the 20th century. This spot is just north of the beginning of today's causeway to Antelope Island. A Church of Jesus Christ of Latter-day Saints meetinghouse sits where a portion of the resort was probably located. (Lynn Arave photograph.)

Terraced mounds of mirabilite, a sodium sulfate mineral, well up as springs and build along Great Salt Lake's shores only in winter and during times of drought, as in this 2022 photograph. Great Salt Lake State Park's south shore marina is on the left, with Stansbury Island and the lake in the distance. (Ray Boren photograph.)

Great Salt Lake's receding shores host one of the largest assemblages of microbialites in the world. The endangered structures, pictured here in Bridger Bay beside Antelope Island but usually under water, are fragile rock-like mounds built by millions of microbes. Microbialites are a primary food source for brine shrimp and brine flies, and thus the lake's entire ecosystem. (Ray Boren photograph.)

Ten

EXPERIENCING THE LAKE TODAY

Unique geology, historic sites, amazing vistas, and adventure await those who visit Great Salt Lake. Here are some ways to experience its wonders:

SALTAIR AND GREAT SALT LAKE STATE PARK. South-shore resorts and beaches were once fabled attractions. Today, not so much. Modern Saltair draws concertgoers and those who want to explore the beach. The state park, marina, beaches, and visitors' center are nearby.

ANTELOPE ISLAND STATE PARK. Great Salt Lake's biggest island is also a park, with a visitors' center, historic ranch, marina, beaches, campgrounds, and trails, as well as wildlife.

STANSBURY ISLAND. Although dominated by evaporation ponds and private lands, the island has an unpaved west-shore road allowing access.

BONNEVILLE SALT FLATS. Interstate 80 rest stops introduce motorists to this vast playa. When the surface is dry, people stroll the flats. A Wendover exit leads to the famed speedway.

FARMINGTON BAY WATERFOWL MANAGEMENT AREA. Depending upon their migratory schedules, waterfowl can be seen year-round here. Other refuges include Ogden Bay, Salt Creek, and the Nature Conservancy's Great Salt Lake Shorelands Preserve.

BEAR RIVER MIGRATORY BIRD REFUGE. Bear River's delta marshes are a federal sanctuary. A visitor center sits beside Interstate 15 in Brigham City, and the refuge lagoons feature a driving loop through bird habitats.

WILLARD BAY STATE PARK AND RESERVOIR. A freshwater adjunct of Great Salt Lake, Willard Bay is a man-made lake, surrounded by earthen dikes, and has two marinas.

GOLDEN SPIKE NATIONAL HISTORICAL PARK. A fascinating site near Great Salt Lake's shores recalls the heyday of the Transcontinental Railroad, featuring the engines *Jupiter* and 119.

ART IN THE LANDSCAPE. Artists discovered an unlikely canvas on Great Salt Lake's fringes. Robert Smithson's 1970 levee, *Spiral Jetty,* at Rozel Point, is a famous example of landscape art. Nancy Holt created her solstice-oriented *Sun Tunnels* near Lucin. Karl Momen designed *Metaphor: Tree of Utah*, a landmark along Interstate 80.

SEEK A HIGH VIEW. A fine way to take in Great Salt Lake's spectacle is to simply go up. Try for window seats on passenger jetliners. If adventurous, tackle the unpaved Davis Skyline Drive. Or motor or hike to a suburban overlook for memorable sunset vistas.

Great Salt Lake fills the horizon during a rain-streaked sunset. Glorious high perspectives of the lake, including Antelope Island, are possible from suburban viewpoints from the Salt Lake area to Brigham City, such as Bountiful Drive, the overlook visited in this 2011 panorama composed of a

Modern Saltair is silhouetted by the setting sun in a 2015 image. This version of the lake's most famous resort, sometimes referred to as "Saltair III," is mainly a concert venue, though many visitors use the site as a trailhead for walks to the receding shore. The classic Saltair pavilions stretched into the lake from the shore a mile to the east. (Ray Boren photograph.)

half-dozen photographs. Adventurous motorists might traverse Davis Skyline Drive. The unpaved forest road follows the Wasatch ridges. (Ray Boren and Robert Noyce photograph.)

As a result of decay and disaster, there have been three incarnations of Saltair. Saltair III, as it is sometimes called, stands on Great Salt Lake's south shore, as in this March 2012 image. The two previous Saltairs both burned down. The third was built in 1981, primarily from salvage of an old Hill Air Force Base hangar. (Ray Boren photograph)

Powered paragliders swoop above Great Salt Lake's south shore, with the ridges of Stansbury Island as a backdrop. The island, often deemed a peninsula, is a mix of public and private land. Accessed via an Interstate 80 interchange near Grantsville, a rough road follows saltworks dikes and the island's west side to the north end's Captain Stansbury Visitors Overlook. Hiking trails along the route offer wonderful viewpoints. (Ray Boren photograph.)

Stansbury Island rises beyond a pool on the south end of Great Salt Lake. The power lines parallel Interstate 80, a major east-west highway. (Note the semi-tractor trailer truck low and in the center.) Stansbury is the lake's second-largest isle. Located in Tooele County, the island is used as a range and for access to salt and mineral evaporation ponds on its south and west sides. (Ray Boren photograph.)

The original adobe Fielding Garr ranch house, on the southeast side of Antelope Island, dates back to 1848, and remained a home until the 1980s. The residence, on the right in this 2012 image, is a centerpiece of the museum-like ranch, which includes a bunkhouse, here on the left; barns and outbuildings, such as a springhouse; and paddocks. Bison often graze nearby. (Ray Boren photograph.)

Schoolchildren frolic in waves at Bridger Bay, located on the north end of Antelope Island State Park, one of the most popular and accessible beaches on Great Salt Lake. The park's visitors' center is nearby, and the location features picnic tables, a seasonal grill, restrooms, and showers. (Lynn Arave photograph.)

Dozens of bald eagles find perches on a wintry day in 2005 at Utah's Farmington Bay Waterfowl Management Area. The refuge, on Great Salt Lake's east shore, is one of many wetland sanctuaries beside or near the inland sea, including sites on Ogden Bay, at Timpie Springs, and at Salt Creek. Great Salt Lake is a major stopover along the migratory Pacific Flyway and Central Flyway. (Ray Boren photograph.)

An unusual feature on Great Salt Lake's northeast side, Willard Bay State Park is a freshwater reservoir, enclosed by a 14.5-mile earthen dike, the Arthur V. Watkins Dam. The water, from the Weber River, is used for irrigation, and the lake, with two marinas, is a popular recreation site, with boating, paddle-boarding, fishing (even in winter), swimming, picnicking, and birdwatching. (Ray Boren photograph.)

On May 10, 1869, Central Pacific and Union Pacific crews and officials met to link eastern and western routes, completing the world's first Transcontinental Railroad with the driving of a "golden spike" at Promontory Summit. Replicas of the locomotives *Jupiter* (No. 60) and No. 119 still do so during re-enactments at the National Park Service's Golden Spike National Historical Park, as on this occasion in 2010. (Ray Boren photograph.)

China Arch, located in Golden Spike National Historical Park, is an intriguing landmark. The Transcontinental Railroad grade is actually visible in this picture, as the view through the arch is looking south. The arch's name may remind visitors that Chinese laborers, working for the Central Pacific Railroad, were important participants in the epic cross-country project. (Ray Boren photograph.)

Utah's Bonneville Raceway, site of numerous world land-speed records over the past century, is on blazingly white salt flats west of Great Salt Lake, near the twin border towns of Wendover, Utah, and West Wendover, Nevada. An Interstate 80 rest stop and a paved roadway to the north offer access to the salt flats, a playa remnant of ancient Lake Bonneville. (Ray Boren photograph.)

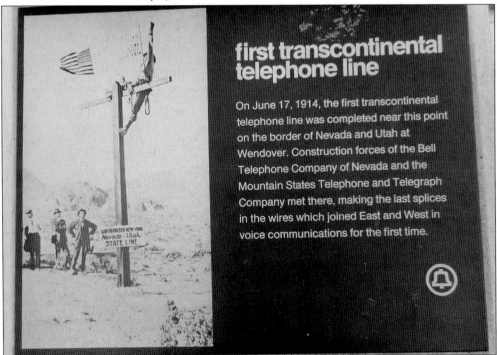

While Great Salt Lake's north end boasts the site where the Transcontinental Railroad was famously completed in 1869, the southwest side boasts another such milestone event—the completion of the first transcontinental telephone line in 1914. Interestingly, in 1861, Western Union's first cross-country telegraph line was also finished in Salt Lake City. (Lynn Arave photograph.)

A June moon rises above salt-encrusted boulders in Great Salt Lake's Rozel Bay in a 2004 night photograph. The frosted rocks are the outer swirls of artist Robert Smithson's *Spiral Jetty*, which surfaced the year before after being submerged and saturated in the hyper-saline northern bay for many years. The renowned earthwork was completed in 1970 by Smithson, who died in a small plane crash in 1973. (Ray Boren photograph.)

Submerged by high water during most of its 50-plus years, Robert Smithson's *Spiral Jetty* has more recently been stranded high and dry in Great Salt Lake's parched Rozel Bay. Since Smithson completed the coiled basalt levee in 1970, it has become one of the most-famous landscape artworks, drawing visitors from around the world to Rozel Point, 15 miles southwest of Golden Spike National Historical Park. (Ray Boren photograph.)

Probably the most visible of the Great Salt Lake region's large-scale artworks is Swedish architect and sculptor Karl Momen's *Metaphor: Tree of Utah.* The multistory creation, completed in 1986, rises suddenly beside Interstate 80 on the vast Bonneville Salt Flats, a concrete pillar topped by six colorful globes layered with native Utah rocks and minerals. (Ray Boren photograph.)

Robert Smithson was not the only artist to consider Great Salt Lake's desert fringes an interesting canvas. His spouse, Nancy Holt, created her *Sun Tunnels* in the 1970s at a remote spot near Lucin, the railroad water stop. Four large concrete tubes are aligned to frame the sun during sunrises and sunsets on the summer and winter solstices, as illustrated here at dawn on June 21, 2002. (Ray Boren photograph.)

BIBLIOGRAPHY

Arave, Lynn. "Fremont Island is no disappointment." *Deseret News* (Salt Lake City, Utah), April 16, 2009.

———. "Great Salt Lake once a summer hot spot." *Deseret News* (Salt Lake City, Utah), August 4, 2006.

Boren, Ray. "Living history: The past comes to life at Antelope Island's Fielding Garr Ranch." *Deseret News* (Salt Lake City, Utah), May 26, 2011.

———. "Time and a place: Utah's Spiral Jetty." *Deseret News* (Salt Lake City, Utah), August 7, 2003.

Czerny, Peter G. *The great Great Salt Lake.* Provo, UT: Brigham Young University Press, 1976.

Fremont, John Charles. *The Exploring Expedition of the Rocky Mountains, Oregon and California* (1843-1844). Washington, DC: US Government, 1849 edition; Project Gutenberg Ebook #9294, 2014.

Huchel, Frederick M. "The Lucin Cutoff." *History of Box Elder County*, 1999. Utah History to Go blog, Utah Department of Cultural & Community Engagement.

Jackson, Richard H., "Great Salt Lake." *Utah History Encyclopedia*, 1994. Utah History to Go blog, Utah Department of Cultural & Community Engagement.

Lyon, Thomas, and Williams, Terry Tempest, eds. *Great and Peculiar Beauty: A Utah Reader.* Salt Lake City, UT: Gibbs Smith, Publisher, 1995.

McCormick, John S. "Saltair." *Utah History Encyclopedia*, 1994. Utah History to Go blog, Utah Department of Cultural & Community Engagement.

Miller, David E. *Great Salt Lake Past and Present.* Salt Lake City, UT: Utah History Atlas, 1992, Weber County Schools Book.

Morgan, Dale L. *The Great Salt Lake.* Indianapolis, IN: Bobbs-Merrill Company, 1947; and Salt Lake City, UT: University of Utah Press, 1995.

Smithson, Robert, and Nancy Holt. Art and estate administered by the Dia Art Foundation: diaart.org.

Stansbury, Howard. *Exploration of the Valley of the Great Salt Lake.* Printed by order of House of Representatives of the United States. Washington, DC: Robert Armstrong, public printer, 1853. Ebook: University of Michigan and Google.

Topping, Gary, et al. "Great Salt Lake." *Utah Historical Quarterly* (Spring 1988 / Volume 56 / Number 2; full issue.)

Van Cott, John W. *Utah Place Names.* Salt Lake City, UT: University of Utah Press, 1990.

DISCOVER THOUSANDS OF LOCAL HISTORY BOOKS FEATURING MILLIONS OF VINTAGE IMAGES

Arcadia Publishing, the leading local history publisher in the United States, is committed to making history accessible and meaningful through publishing books that celebrate and preserve the heritage of America's people and places.

Find more books like this at
www.arcadiapublishing.com

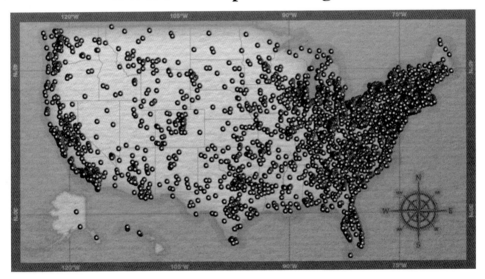

Search for your hometown history, your old stomping grounds, and even your favorite sports team.

Consistent with our mission to preserve history on a local level, this book was printed in South Carolina on American-made paper and manufactured entirely in the United States. Products carrying the accredited Forest Stewardship Council (FSC) label are printed on 100 percent FSC-certified paper.

MADE IN THE USA